CRACKING
the
Coconut
Code

Other Books by
Mary Jo McCabe

• • •

*Learn to See: An Approach to Your
Inner Voice Through Symbols*

Come This Way: A Better Life Awaits

It All Begins Here: Interpreting Your Dreams

CRACKING
the
Coconut
Code

7 Insights to
Transform Your Life

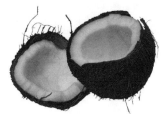

Mary Jo McCabe

Princess Books
New York, NY

Published in the United States by: Princess Books, a Division of Get Psych'd, Inc., New York, NY

Distributed in the United States by: Hay House, Inc., P.O. Box 5100, Carlsbad, CA 92018-5100 • *Phone:* (760) 431-7695 or (800) 654-5126 • *Fax:* (760) 431-6948 or (800) 650-5115 • www.hayhouse.com • *Distributed in Australia by:* Hay House Australia Pty. Ltd., 18/36 Ralph St., Alexandria NSW 2015 • *Phone:* 612-9669-4299 • *Fax:* 612-9669-4144 • www.hayhouse.com.au • *Distributed in the United Kingdom by:* Hay House UK, Ltd. • Unit 62, Canalot Studios • 222 Kensal Rd., London W10 5BN • *Phone:* 44-20-8962-1230 • *Fax:* 44-20-8962-1239 • www.hayhouse.co.uk • *Distributed in the Republic of South Africa by:* Hay House SA (Pty), Ltd., P.O. Box 990, Witkoppen 2068 • *Phone/Fax:* 2711-7012233 • orders@psdprom.co.za • *Distributed in Canada by:* Raincoast • 9050 Shaughnessy St., Vancouver, B.C. V6P 6E5 • *Phone:* (604) 323-7100 • *Fax:* (604) 323-2600

Editorial supervision: Jill Kramer   *Design:* Jenny Richards

Library of Congress Cataloging-in-Publication Data

McCabe, Mary Jo.
  Cracking the coconut code : 7 insights to transform your life / Mary Jo McCabe.
    p. cm.
  ISBN 1-932128-11-5 (hardcover)
  1. Self-realization—Miscellanea. 2. Spiritualism. I. Title.
  BF1275.S44M33 2005
  158.1—dc22

                    2004018686

              ISBN 13: 978-1-932128-11-6
              ISBN 10: 1-932128-11-5

          07 06 05 04   4 3 2 1
          1st printing, December 2004

        Printed in the United States of America

CONTENTS

FOREWORD

For the last 20 years, I've been helping people communicate with their loved ones on the Other Side. Now whether you believe in that ability or not, it's extremely healing to be able to *know* that there's another place where the soul goes after the physical body ceases to sustain life. Even if you're skeptical about that process, I'm sure you've questioned or thought about the existence of some type of Heaven . . . or your own soul.

But let's not worry about what's next at this moment; let's worry about your soul *now*. I've seen so many people over the last two decades spend their time wondering about what's coming next that they potentially miss out on what's currently happening in their lives. And I've had the experience of people coming to me in the hopes that someone on the Other Side is going to "fix" their lives for them.

Whether it's to find a new relationship, lose weight, attract wealth, or get a better job, I've heard it all: "Will I be rich? Will I find love? Will I ever lose weight?" These are questions that constantly plague our society.

I've often said that we live in this fast-food world where people would, if they could, drive up to the window to place their "life order," and by the time they'd finished driving around the building, they would have gotten married, lost 50 pounds, and become a millionaire

—just like that! That's not reality, though. Life is certainly not to be equated with a hamburger . . . but instead, a coconut.

When I first met Mary Jo McCabe almost ten years ago, I was impressed by her generosity of spirit: She didn't know me, yet she was all too eager to welcome me into her city and help me promote a seminar. By some people's standards, I would have been her "competition," coming in to "steal" her clients. Instead, I was met with warmth and unconditional friendship, which has lasted for the entire decade I've known her. What struck me immediately was her blunt, up-front, and honest approach to her work. What you see is exactly what you get.

Over the years, I've had the opportunity to lecture with Mary Jo across the United States and watch first-hand how people react to her teachings. She doesn't lecture *at* others; she discusses her message *with* them. It didn't matter if there were 50 people in the room with us or 5,000—that impressed me. She was just sharing with, and helping, others.

When Mary Jo and I spoke about this book, and she passionately told me how she wanted to help people stop surrendering their desires to some unhelpful future—and show them how they could get to the milk in their own life's coconut—I was moved to be a part of that process of transition.

I know this is a book that will help you transform your thinking, and ultimately, your present, to shape the future you know you want to create. So read the book, follow the insights, crack the code, and be like all the celebrities in those ads who ask you if you've got milk! But know it's your *life's milk* that you're enjoying. Once you've found success, share the code and help others in the same way that Mary Jo has helped you.

— **John Edward**

● ● ●   ● ● ●

PREFACE
Why You?
Why Me?

A few years ago, a woman asked me how I developed my ability to interpret symbols. She was essentially wondering how I hear my soul's voice, or the voice of God. No one had ever posed that question before, and it stunned me because I'd never really thought about it. It was almost as if someone had inquired how I learned to breathe, because listening to my soul's voice is so natural to my daily existence. To me, this voice always felt more like a part of who I was, an extension of my personality and purpose in life. After I shared my thoughts with her, this woman asked, "If you're not aware of the process you used, can you at least teach me how I can hear my own soul's voice?"

Immediately, I saw a coconut. I explained to her what that symbol meant to me: A coconut is loved for its tasty white "meat" and rich, sweet milk, but one must get through its thick, tough shell to reach its reward. For the life of me, I couldn't understand why this applied to her question. But before I could go on, she inquired, "So how do you get to the milk in the coconut?"

I realized that her question was intended to make me think, and that my job was to try to figure out why I was shown this symbol. I asked for further explanation and received the following seven insights to help people transform their lives—in effect, to reach the milk of the coconut:

1. Overcome the fear of knowing
2. Understand the history of emotional tangles
3. Identify property
4. Support
5. Embrace shortcomings
6. Focus
7. Diminish occupation

I had absolutely no clue what these seven insights meant, nor did I realize the importance of what they represented. Since that time, however, I've analyzed these phrases extensively and have discussed them with my family members, friends, and clients to help me interpret their meaning. I wanted to know what the underlying messages were so that I could be the conduit to those thirsty for the answer. (Although I didn't know the insights by name until then, I came to realize that they'd always been a part of my life.)

Yet before I discuss what will allow you to begin "Cracking the Coconut Code," let me share the journey that has allowed me to bring my work to you.

Learning to Crack Coconuts

For the last three decades, I've been helping individuals recognize how they can find their purpose and get more out of their lives. My mission has been to shed light on the everyday signs and symbols that God puts in my clients' lives, and then to teach them how to recognize their own messages. In other words, I'm an interpreter of symbols, or an "intuitive."

Skeptical? Good. Afraid? Don't be. I really am normal (or so people tell me!). I do not now, nor have I ever, owned a crystal ball, and I retired my blue eye shadow in the '80s with the rest of the country. I don't intend to get mystical on you; instead, I want to be your teacher so that I can share what I've learned with you and help you get the greatest fulfillment out of life.

I believe that we all have the ability to communicate with our soul or inner voice, that part of us that's essentially God's voice. I know that we can bring peace into our lives by listening to and letting God guide us through life. *How?* you may wonder. Well, I refer to the process of listening to your soul's voice and transforming your life as "Cracking the Coconut Code." Of course it's an analogy, but it defines how I learned to listen to my own inner voice.

Try to imagine your soul as a coconut, and the rewards of life as the milk inside it. The more skilled you are at cracking the shell, the more milk you'll retain for greater nourishment. Your life provides you with the lessons you'll need to break open that husk—the more you live your life in a spiritual manner, the better you become at cracking open your own self and savoring life's rewards.

My work has led me to share my knowledge with you so that you may also see the coconut (your soul) for what it truly is: a precious object that contains a fabulous reward inside a tough, protective shell.

As many of us learn along our paths, it's not always the destination but the journey that provides us with the greatest learning. My own path began rather humbly: I never imagined that I'd end up leading a life that was so nontraditional. After all, who spends her days as a child wishing that she was intuitive, leading to a career path that will bring forth such varied opinions from friends, colleagues, and even total strangers?

Today I'm thankful that I trusted my faith to lead me on the journey I was to take, which has allowed me to realize my potential, to engage in a profession that many consider outside the realm of normal, and ultimately, to bring it into the mainstream.

My Younger Years

I was born a twin, the oldest of the pair and the second of four daughters. My childhood was normal, or so it seemed to me. I wouldn't describe my family as well-off, but one thing I always had was my faith. I always felt that there was a force greater than I who was looking out for me. I now realize that the faith instilled in me as a child is what carried me through all the obstacles that I encountered along my path.

I can remember having experiences as a young girl that some may describe as "different." For example, having dreams at night that played out in front of me the next day was not unusual for me. In fact, I thought that these nighttime dramas were so common that I never even shared them with my twin. I just assumed that she also had dreams played out in front of her. (I've since come to learn that this type of experience *is* normal for all of us, if we pay attention to it.)

One night when I was a teenager reciting my prayers, I saw a man sitting on a rock in a wooded area. What I perceived was so clear that I could best describe it as "a vision." This man was draped in a white robe; had beautiful, curly hair; and carried a staff. I opened my eyes and said, "Oh! I think I just saw God!" I understand now that while this man was certainly a godly being, he was probably one of my spiritual guides. At the time, I remember feeling a strong sense of peace emanating from him. In fact, I felt more comfortable with him than I did in my own world.

Looking back on this experience of *thinking* I saw God (silly me), I was probably reaching for the star on top of the tree when I should have been paying attention to the tiny ornament in front of me. In other words, although the message was from God, the messenger wasn't God Himself. While my first inclination was to focus on my interpretation of the vision, I believe that the purpose of this experience was to show me that I wasn't alone— I did indeed have support on a spiritual level. I've since relied on this support many times for courage and comfort, so this was a very important event for me.

Throughout my childhood and early-adult years, these dreams continued, becoming more intense and meaningful. They often foretold important events in my life, progressing to the point that I began to trust them, thereby strengthening my faith in God. I suppose the old adage holds that "normal is what normal is to you." I now realize that these early experiences were paving a way that I'd later rely on, trusting my own soul's voice to prepare me to answer my own calling.

A Turning Point

By sharing what I've gone through, I hope to show you that while individual growth and experience has immediate meaning, it's part of the overall plan of your life—that is, it's instrumental to you as you transform your life in the long run, not for the short term.

While my earliest experiences were definitely eye-opening, my reflection helped me see them as important building blocks, allowing me to understand and accept the events that would continue in my life. My early adulthood was about as mainstream as you could get: I got married, had a child, and was active in my husband's career and my son's life. My husband, Jim, was an Air Force officer, and I embraced my role as a source of support for the family. We had the opportunity to live in some great places all over the U.S., and every time we moved, I had the opportunity to learn about each destination . . . and in the process, found out so much about myself as well. However, one place made a dramatic and lasting impression on me that really changed my view of the world.

We were stationed in the Philippines in the late '70s, during a time when the country was divided into the super wealthy and the very poor. Many members of the surrounding communities worked on the military base, and I took advantage of their presence to learn about their culture and way of life. At the time, I could never have imagined the impact that they'd have on me. I was able to see how much or how little most of these people had, yet they were generally happy and peaceful. Their faith was the core of their existence, and their main goal in life was to make sure that their children were educated in order to better their lives and to care for their older relatives within the extended family unit.

Witnessing this unconditional love amid such meager living conditions would become a building block in the foundation upon which I built my spiritual journey. It was also during this time that I began to focus inward on my own lessons, my own obstacles—not those of Mary Jo the intuitive, but those of Mary Jo, the woman, the wife, and the mother. This period of personal growth served as a catalyst to clear the path for what lay before me.

Although my religion has always been a large part of my life, the *spirituality* of religion is what really drew me in. My husband and I were very active in the Catholic church and lived our lives consistent with its teachings; however, this didn't come without confusion. I had quite a questioning spirit and always wanted to know more— to know what lay beneath the surface, or what was "behind the curtain," so to speak. I just felt that there was more to the equation.

My biggest question concerned confession. I felt that God was with me every day, and I thought I'd developed a good dialogue with Him, so why did I need to introduce a priest into this relationship?

The priest I asked this of grew very frustrated with me. He pointed to a bird outside and said, "That bird has wings, but do you see me questioning God as to why that bird has wings? No! I just accept that it is so, and that is what you need to do." He obviously could have handled this situation better, but his response led me to realize that there were some answers I'd have to find out for myself.

It's amazing that this innocent exchange made such an impact on me, because a few years later, I began my own journey, with a sense of acceptance of my own experiences. This then redefined my life and put me on a more spiritual path.

● ● ●

I'm a firm believer that people are in our lives for a reason, more than likely to further our personal and spiritual development. (In fact, don't think for one second that you're holding this book by accident.) We are where we are in each moment of every day for a purpose, for a lesson. This could not have been more true for me.

Before we lived in the Phillipines, the Air Force transferred us to San Antonio, Texas, a strong Catholic and military community. There, I met Susan, the wife of another officer, at a birthday party that our sons were attending.

As our sons became friends, so did we, spending time discussing our belief systems. Susan shared her experiences with me about her study group, which was reading the works of Edgar Cayce, an early pioneer in the field of metaphysics. Cayce was one of the original intuitives of this century and was widely known for his ability to channel health remedies while in sleeplike trances. (His work is still significant today because of his early homeopathic remedies.) He was very religious, and his faith was never broken by the fears and doubts of others—that is, he stayed true to his path. His life was, and still is, an inspiration for me.

Susan encouraged me to read Cayce's writings and invited me to attend her study group so that I could learn more about him. In the process, my new friend helped bring my early experiences into the mainstream, "normalizing" my dreams, and in turn, further strengthening my belief in them. She was the first person who didn't judge me and who understood my beliefs. She allowed me to question myself in a true learning environment.

Soon I had my first tremendous breakthrough. One night I had a dream that I was alone in a hospital waiting area. I remember that I was facing swinging doors when they slowly opened. In walked a woman who I thought resembled the charismatic faith healer Katherine Kuhlman. I remember questioning why I'd be dreaming about this woman, since I wasn't a follower or a fan of her work. Nevertheless, she continued walking toward me. She looked to be about 30 years old, and she was wearing a dated, green-flowered chiffon dress. She was followed by several figures in white robes, but I couldn't see their faces because white hoods covered them. As she moved toward me, she delivered a message about my husband: "Jim is already there."

She then leaned forward and exhaled three deep breaths on my head. I saw and felt myself melt into a puddle on the chair. The sensation I had was divine, and I've never felt anything quite like it since. The next morning, I remembered thinking again, *Why would Katherine Kuhlman visit me in a dream? I don't even follow her work.* (In fact, I didn't even know that she was deceased until after I had this dream.) I also remembered thinking, *What in the world did she mean about my husband being "there"? Where was "there" exactly, and why wasn't I with him?*

I wanted to know what she was referring to, but you must understand that most questions in life are responded to when we're ready to hear and accept them, not necessarily when we want the answers. So my queries weren't immediately answered, but I did know that this dream was bathed in a sense of peacefulness. As a result, I realized that its underlying message was meant to provide comfort to me once again and to remind me that I wasn't alone.

My dreams continued both day and night. It seemed that each time I closed my eyes, I saw unfamiliar faces, young and old, happy and sad. I had no idea who these people were or why I saw them. Thankfully, I never felt frightened—not once did it occur to me that I should be afraid. I was confident in my faith, and I trusted, as I always have, that whatever happened within me was safe and connected to God.

My dreams intrigued me. I wished to understand them and to know why they were coming to me, so I turned to the things that were familiar: my own belief system and my faith. As a practicing Catholic, I'd come to rely on the rosary when I needed strength and guidance, so I turned again to it for understanding, protection, and direction. I wanted to understand God's intentions for me. While I already knew that my path was different from others, I now realized that my very *life* was changing, and I needed to embrace this new role and responsibility.

However, it would be years of searching and learning before I'd understand how I needed to transform my own life and to crack what I now refer to as the Coconut Code. Remember, the journey contains more learning than the destination ever could. My own path seemed to have a new and strange experience around each corner. However, the next one was completely unexpected and changed my life forever.

A Life-Changing Experience

It was 1980. We'd just returned from the Philippines, and were living in Illinois in a small military community across the river from St. Louis, Missouri. I didn't envision this as a place where I'd have my first hint of what God's plan was for me. To be consistent with everything I'd ever read about spiritual awakenings, I would have envisioned it to be on a mountaintop during a sunset rather than in a suburban living room in a town surrounded by cornfields. Nothing could have prepared me for I was about to see.

In a dream that was more vivid than any before, I was straddling a fence. I saw a "blur" of ice-blue energy on one side of the fence and a woman on the other. This "blur" was speaking to me, and I relayed the message to the woman on the other side of the fence. I couldn't understand why they couldn't communicate with each other. They were right across the fence from each other, so why did they need me? While at the time I didn't understand the purpose of the dream, I now realize that it was a foreshadowing of my life's path—that of a communicator, an interpreter, a teacher, and a conduit between the spiritual and the physical. Thankfully, in that same year, the message was clarified, and it was marked by another meaningful event.

My husband was out of town on a military assignment, and I was cleaning the house, the unenviable job of every homemaker. While vacuuming the living room, I was overcome with a need to sit down and meditate. Because I'd begun to trust the information that I was receiving from my dreams, I didn't question the feeling—to be honest, it was so strong that I didn't even give it a second thought. However, let me be clear here: I am *not* the meditating type—I'm rather energetic and can't sit still for long, so the thought of meditation wasn't an appealing one. Since I was alone, I said aloud, "Okay, you have 15 minutes!"

I abandoned the vacuum cleaner and took a seat on the sofa, and as soon as I closed my eyes, I saw myself in a classroom. I was hurrying to get to a desk, and as I took my seat, a huge man appeared before me and said, "You have now entered *our* world." Let me reiterate: He was a *huge* man, and immediately I thought that this person needed to go on a diet. I then realized that he was the Buddha, and I felt guilty for being judgmental. I'd later realize that lessons come in all shapes and sizes, and they're not for me or anyone else to judge. After all, we experience what we need to learn. . . .

I was so startled that my eyes flew open, as if someone had hit me on the back of the head. This vision seemed so foreign to me because all I knew was that the Buddha represented Buddhism, which wasn't a religion I knew anything about. When I came to my senses, I immediately jumped up and called my husband. I told him about the vision and explained that I thought I needed to learn about Buddhism. Jim, in his stoic way, said, "Good God, don't tell anybody. This needs to stay between us."

At the time, Jim was president of the Catholic Parish Council, and he must have wondered how in the world we were going to fit Buddhism into our lives. Poor guy— he must have been terrified! You have to understand that in 1980, in a small, conservative military town in Illinois, there weren't very many Buddhists. On top of that, it wasn't common practice to have anything spiritual in your life unless you received it in church, let alone practice another religion!

I was wondering how I was going to bring this up at the next Catholic picnic! Imagine this: *After I drop off my green-bean casserole to Sister Mary Francis, I then mosey on over to the pavilion, where I announce that the McCabes are off to the Far East to meet my Buddha!* Can you picture everyone's reactions if I'd done this? It's a good thing I didn't, but I *was* tempted. I'm always up for a good laugh.

Until this point, my dreams seemed really normal. I could understand their lessons without much effort. However, this last dream of the Buddha was completely off my radar screen. I knew I wasn't crazy, so there had to be a lesson here. I needed to find that lesson, so I had homework to do! I began reading books on Buddhism, discreetly browsing the library, hoping that no one would ever discover me crouched down between the stacks where books on the Buddha were filed away.

What I uncovered was so enlightening, and not the least bit threatening to my Catholic faith; I could embrace this lesson. I learned that meditation is an excellent means to clear the clutter in one's mind and connect with oneself, and that the ultimate goal of Buddhism is to attain inner peace. Well, isn't that what we all want? I realized then that I didn't need to convert, but I did need to apply this lesson to further my spiritual journey. In the words of His Holiness the 14th Dalai Lama: "Don't try to use what you learn from Buddhism to be a Buddhist; use it to be a better whatever-you-already-are."

• • •

I'm grateful to my husband for always being so supportive of my experiences. He could have easily dismissed me as a kook. After all, what we were going through wasn't "by the book," and there was no precedent in our lives for such lunacy. If you knew Jim, you'd never confuse him with a metaphysical person. He's very spiritual, and his faith is very important to him, but this change in his life—and in his wife—had to be a shocking experience. Nevertheless, instead of judging me, he was supportive. My husband is one of the greatest people I know, and one of the world's most solid human beings. What you see with him is what you get, and he's certainly not shy about his views on anything.

I'm sure it was, and still is, difficult for him to be married to someone who loves living on the edge. But my good friend Susan laughs when she thinks about all this. As she says, "You add color to his life, and he'd be bored to tears if he didn't have you." Looking back, the Katherine Kuhlman dream revealed that Jim was already there, so maybe he's always been with me to support me on this journey. As I write this, I realize that the spiritual lesson I need to learn in this lifetime is one that he's already mastered. That's quite a hard pill to swallow for any wife.

Anyway, I was so confused, because my experiences were becoming more frequent and more intense. And based on that last dream, I thought I was supposed to follow Buddhism. Therefore, I scheduled an appointment with a meditation instructor to learn the basics. For me, learning how to meditate was a necessary tool if I wanted to become a good student.

The instructor came to our home for my one and only lesson, and I'm sure he never thought that this appointment would turn out the way it did. I need to say right off the bat that this man didn't like me, nor I him—we were two people who simply had a job to do. I felt that he was pompous and too much into his ego; however, I knew he had something I wanted—the basics of meditation.

During my lesson, my nine-year-old son, Bhrett, sat and watched as the instructor walked me through the meditation process. As we sat around the kitchen table, he told me to close my eyes, take three deep breaths, and recite the Lord's Prayer for strength and protection. The next step felt uncomfortable, even for me. He asked me to hum "Om" three times. While I was "Omming," I started wondering, *What is Bhrett thinking about this?* and *What if Jim walked in here right now? Mary Jo, you better hurry up and get to the meat on this bone!* So I did everything the instructor told me to do. After my initial entrance into the meditation, he asked me to relax and enjoy the space I'd created within myself. This is where it all began.

What I saw was nothing less than astounding: The profile of a man was standing before me, so clear and real that I could vividly see his porcelain-like skin. He was wearing a gray cashmere sweater, his hair was a beautiful silver, and his face was as smooth and slick as a ribbon. It felt as if I were having a one-on-one meeting with him even though he wasn't physically in front of me. The interesting thing about this experience was that

I was aware of everything around me—my son, my instructor, and the man in the meditation. I was able to concentrate and communicate simultaneously in both realms. I remember feeling more in tune with myself than I ever had before.

This man identified himself as Dr. Woods. I'm not sure how I knew this, nor did I understand the significance of his name—I was so overwhelmed that I couldn't grasp how any of this was working. I wasn't afraid of him; rather, I had this overwhelming feeling of unconditional love and complete acceptance.

I remember asking the instructor how I knew what Dr. Woods was saying because he wasn't moving his mouth. He told me that he was communicating with me telepathically. Dr. Woods went on to tell me that he was one of my son's spiritual guides, and I relayed his messages to my instructor and Bhrett.

When the session ended, 30 minutes had passed. Although it seemed to last only seconds, I couldn't remember what was said during the meditation. All I could remember was the love Dr. Woods displayed for my son—truly unconditional love. I knew that this experience would change my life forever; I just wasn't sure how.

The Guides

Initially, I wanted to share my experience with my family and friends. What was I thinking? I realized I was a bit naïve to think that this would be openly accepted, so I decided to call one close girlfriend, Pauline, with whom I'd shared these things in the past. Pauline was also the wife of an Air Force officer and a devout Catholic. We'd shared our thoughts on faith, spirituality, and religion many times, and I knew that she'd be a great support for me.

When she came over, Pauline asked me to meditate to see if I could repeat what I'd done the night before. We sat down, I closed my eyes, took three deep breaths, and recited the Lord's Prayer. This time, I omitted the "Omming" because it just wasn't for me. Amazingly, the same thing happened, but this time Dr. Woods told me that he didn't work alone. He said that he worked with a group of individuals, collectively referred to as the "The Guides." I couldn't see them, but I could feel their presence because they emanated a strong sense of unconditional love.

It would be ten years before I actually saw them all. When they did reveal themselves to me, 25 to 30 white-robed figures were standing in an open meadow, looking quite reverent and wise. I realized that I'd met them once before, briefly, in my dream of Katherine Kuhlman. It humbled me to realize how many of them it took to deliver a message, and how much it means to the Universe for each and every one of us to have a better understanding of who and what we are.

Pauline and I continued to work on my meditation process for two years. As we continued our sessions, these meditations evolved into more of a trancelike state. I'd close my eyes, and the information would come through me so fast. My voice was loud, with a strong Irish accent; my body was active; and my emotions were quite variable. *(Reader, please don't put this book down, and don't be afraid—this is as strange as it gets!)* During this state, I would be given information concerning a person's life, which very often included insight into their family members, relationships, personal challenges, and life struggles. Later, The Guides would further explain these messages, stating that they were intended to guide people to live a more meaningful, purposeful, and spiritual life.

Now you're probably wondering if this book is going to make you have visions or become a channeler. Don't worry—you won't (unless it's a part of your life path). You have to understand that my purpose in this life is to *teach what I've learned*. I had to have these experiences so that I could reach an understanding of the lessons of our souls and see the true connection to God in order to teach others. In teaching you about my work, I hope that you'll understand the importance of recognizing and researching your own lessons. In doing so, you'll become a student who's able to answer your own call, find your own true path, and hear your soul's voice.

As a student of my own life, I noticed that things were evolving. The Guides taught me the importance of universal signs and symbols, a language that would become our means of communication. They'd show me a symbol, and I'd interpret what it meant to me. This was how I built my symbol "dictionary." I then started to share my experiences with a very close group of friends at the Air Force base where Jim was stationed. They didn't think I was a nutcase (at least not to my face), and their acceptance allowed me the freedom to expand and explore my gift. They confirmed that the messages provided meaning and were accurate within their lives. It became clear that these readings were actually the sparks that could ignite a person's inner journey.

Moving Toward Acceptance

The acceptance that I have today hasn't come without some difficulty and self-doubt, as well as sharp ridicule. I needed to be prepared to handle the criticism of others, along with *my* lingering doubts concerning my life path. During a difficult time, I consulted my husband's cousin, an ordained Roman Catholic priest, and I openly shared my experiences. I told him that I'd never asked for this gift, so should I continue on this journey?

His message to me was simple and beautiful. He boldly asked, "Does it strengthen your faith in God?" When I confirmed that it did, he simply stated, "Then don't let anyone tell you that it's wrong."

I'm sure this was the first time that someone had approached him with this "problem." Regardless, his honesty and acceptance shed light on my life path, giving me the greatest gift that anyone ever could—an understanding of God that made sense.

From that day forward, I moved ahead, knowing that if I continued to develop my gift, a better life awaited me. I knew that I needed to cultivate the fields before me.

Nothing would come easy, but I also knew that if I had faith, I'd continue to answer my calling, so I kept sharing my experiences with my close inner circle of family members and friends.

Looking back, I have to laugh at some of those experiences. My sisters were concerned that I was hearing voices, seeing visions, and worst of all, sharing them with people in the community. They worried that people would call the paddy wagon to haul me off to the asylum. "Poor Bhrett," they said, "his mother has gone nuts." Consequently, they all agreed that my youngest sister, Joy, needed to come for a "visit" to determine if I needed to see a psychiatrist or to spend some time in the hospital.

When Joy and her husband, Stan, arrived, they asked me to "do what you do." When I was finished, they were speechless, but they quickly confirmed that I wasn't psychotic; rather, the messages that I was communicating were profound. In fact, Stan, a stoic and an admitted skeptic about such experiences, later shared that this visit "reopened and reconfirmed" his faith in God.

● ● ●

This has definitely been a learning process for my family and me, progressing from small circles of friends to an established practice in Baton Rouge, Louisiana, where we initially moved to be closer to my twin sister, Jean, in Florida. Jim retired from the Air Force and tried to get back into his earlier profession, pharmacy. We were working hard to become part of the civilian world.

After being part of military life and having such close, family-like friends, Jim and I felt scared and alone, so I decided to find a job and maybe meet some new people. I'd worked as a model for an upscale department store in St. Louis that was eventually sold to Dillard's, so I sent the Dillard's in Baton Rouge my letter of recommendation and résumé for part-time employment. I knew that they didn't have modeling work, but I just wanted a job. I needed to be around new faces in order to feel at home in Baton Rouge, and we needed the money.

So, after being hired in the cosmetics department, I told a few of my co-workers about my gift, and it wasn't long before the word was out. My secret life was moving to the forefront.

Delivering Messages, Receiving Gifts

When word of mouth about what I was doing circulated, I began to receive phone calls day and night from people wanting readings. I soon discovered that I didn't need to have the individual in my physical presence to read for them—I could do "my thing" over the telephone. It got to the point where I had to set aside three hours every Tuesday and Thursday from 6 P.M. to 9 P.M. to answer phone calls . . . unfortunately, they started coming in several hours before, to several hours after, that time slot.

I initially didn't charge for these sessions because I felt that I was only the conduit and shouldn't profit from the messages I was delivering. However, in order to remain professional and salvage my personal life, I realized that it was imperative to establish an office. So in 1987, I formed The McCabe Institute, Inc., and started booking scheduled appointments without an ounce of advertising. As word of mouth grew, so did the demand for personal readings.

I insist that individuals don't *need* to come back to see me a second time because very often the messages they're given are life lasting. Obviously, people like to return when they have a particular question or need advice on a major event in their lives. I encourage them, as well as my readers, to develop their own intuitive abilities so that they can receive their own messages and begin to explore their lives on a spiritual level. As this book will clearly demonstrate, you can learn to receive your own messages—that is, crack your own coconut and drink your own milk.

●　●　●

My development has been a process, and I'm constantly working to better my life by listening to the messages given to me. I strongly believe that we all have the ability to be intuitive, but I also recognize that we must work at it on a daily basis. It's similar to playing a piano, which many of us can master to some degree or another. Some of us practice and practice to prepare for recitals—

some with phenomenal talent and others with limited skill—while others play beautifully without practicing but may not reach their potential. And then there are some who have the God-given talent to play the piano in enormous concert halls and make it seem that their music is coming from the wings of angels. Likewise, I feel that I've been blessed with a gift that I should share with others, and even though I know that some might ridicule me or be skeptical, I have faith in my skills, faith in my God-chosen life path, and faith in the journey that I've followed in order to be where I am today.

Many of my clients over the past 20 years have told me that their lives have been changed for the better by the information they've received through their personal and group readings, and from the material in my books. Consistently, they tell me that they've been able to identify and face obstacles that hinder their spiritual and emotional growth.

Note, however, that *I am not, never have been, nor ever will be, a therapist.* In my readings, I simply interpret the messages given to me. Once I begin to put my own "two cents" in, I distort the message, so I've learned to remove myself from the communication. Think back to the old exercise in school when one by one we whispered a secret to our neighbor. Did the message remain intact by the end of the chain? Never! So my job is to step back and let the message come through.

Throughout my personal and professional growth, I've been fortunate to meet some great people. I've also encountered some whom I wish never to meet again, but it's been the latter individuals I've learned the most from in my work. I consider myself an open target, particularly for those who don't understand my work. This was actually shown to me in my own neighborhood one day. My neighbor and I were having lunch, and I gave her a copy of one of my earliest books, *Come This Way*. I was very proud of it and wanted to share it with her. Later she called and asked to come over. We were sitting outside, and she began by asking me, "Why do you speak about 'The Guides'? Don't you mean 'The Gods'?"

I replied, "What do you mean?"

She said, "You've replaced God in your life for these 'Guides.'"

I have to admit that I was dumbfounded because the entire book was about having and embracing God in your life! The Guides are teachers, which is a very important point. And Webster's defines a *teacher* as someone who tells or shows the fundamentals of something.

I explained to my neighbor my belief that we're all a part of God, that The Guides are my teachers, and that they trained me to communicate with the part of us that God created in His own likeness—the soul. But I don't even think she listened! She went on to say that if I followed what I'd written in my book, then I was turning my back on religion and spreading false truths.

Again, I explained to her my belief that spirituality is an expression of God, which manifests itself in life every day. To forget that is to turn your back on your soul. To get closer to God, you should want to embrace your soul and work to discover your life's purpose. It's like a song you knew from long ago—it's that familiar feeling you try to place but can't quite understand how. Spirituality doesn't contradict religious teachings; in fact, they go together like red beans and rice. You can have both in your life. My neighbor listened quietly, and I thought she understood my position on this subject. Silly me!

A few months later at a neighborhood Christmas party, a man approached me and began to ask questions about my work. What started as an innocent conversation became an hour-long, heated discussion with neither of us getting anywhere. He didn't hear a thing I said, and I failed to grow horns on my head and spout fire. I was extremely shaken by his belittling of my work, and I considered this an attack on my character. I excused myself and went home. Later, I learned from another neighbor that several residents had chosen him as a spokesperson to try to expel the "demon" (their word, not mine) from the neighborhood. It didn't work.

Since that experience, I've carefully chosen with whom and where I spend my time. In the beginning, The Guides told me that I was never to lead anyone to my work, and that people who needed me would find me. Unfortunately, I learned this lesson the hard way. I now think twice before offering unsolicited advice or books to anyone! Yet for every bad story, please know that there are a hundred good ones, and these are what keep me focused on my path.

The most startling questions that I've been asked are: "What gives you the authority to do what you do?"

and "How can you teach workshops and offer information without a degree?" This hurts, but as I've explained many times, I'm neither a therapist nor a minister—I'm simply a student of The Guides' teachings. The Guides were, and still are, my professors. I hope that what I've learned helps me teach, and at the same time helps others learn from my work. I believe that as I continue to develop my gifts and skills, I'm fortunate enough to be my own skeptic. My advice to you is to do the same—after all, skepticism is part of the earliest form of learning.

In looking back at my life, I realize that the seven insights discussed in this book enabled me to find my path and helped me transform my life. I've applied them to daily issues and to my life as a whole. I hope that you'll appreciate them as much as I do, and that you'll find the path you're seeking.

Now, as you're reading this book and beginning your journey, you're validating my true work. More than anything, I want you to find *your* purpose and know *your* soul. I know that you will see the transformation in the world around you once you begin Cracking the Coconut Code.

● ● ●   ● ● ●

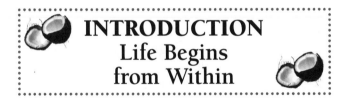

INTRODUCTION
Life Begins
from Within

By now, you know that my work involves interpreting the symbolic language that I've built with The Guides. However, in order for you to build your own symbolic language, you must first understand that *you have both a physical self __and__ a spiritual self.* This is the most important sentence in this book. It's very important for me that you clearly understand this concept so that you'll be able to begin the process of hearing your soul's voice.

Think of it this way: The spiritual self, your soul, is hidden from the naked eye. This part of you is made in God's likeness—it knows all about you, it knows what's best for you, and it knows how to help you receive from life what you truly need. In other words, it's the real you. Think of your soul as an ancient, wise teacher who looks after your well-being and provides daily direction and guidance for your life. Your soul has remarkable patience, love, devotion, and faith in you and is always steering you to follow the unique path God chose for you.

The physical self is what others see and is open to the outside world, and this includes your emotions. It's similar to the tough outer husk of the coconut, which protects the milk and nourishment in the center. Every day your ego lives and functions around the negative trappings of the physical world, such as greed, jealousy, and selfish motivations, to name just a few. If you become tangled in such things, they can rot your shell and erode your physical self, making your spiritual self vulnerable. If you live life without any regard for your spiritual self by devoting too much attention to the desires of the physical self, you will lead a life of dissatisfaction, frustration, emptiness, and self-doubt. Unfortunately, this sets a pattern that can take years or lifetimes to overcome in order to regain the needed balance.

Your goal is to blend your spiritual self and your physical self into complete balance with each other. They'll then function as one but will still retain their own uniqueness. As you maintain a healthy equilibrium between them, your development and lessons will come much easier. If you live life with either part of you overpowering the other, your journey will be much more difficult. Your life will be off-kilter.

For example, there are so many people consumed with making money that they're unable to prioritize the important things in life. These individuals often look back with regret because of the relationships they neglected. As you know, life isn't just about making money. Now this doesn't mean that wealth can't be had—but it does mean that your spiritual self will constantly pull your physical self to maintain balance. Therefore, it's about the relationships and lessons we learn while making money—or the journey, not the destination. Life is about that equilibrium, and those individuals who effectively balance their physical and spiritual demands often remain the most grounded. Until your life is in sync, you'll never experience the fullness of it.

Likewise, if you immerse yourself completely in your spiritual self, you'll neglect your physical needs. This imbalance creates what I refer to as a "spiritual beatnik," in which someone becomes so immersed in their spiritual journey that they become a walking billboard for the New Age. Their persona revolves around everything metaphysical, such as crystals, candles, and anything that may be advertised or suggested to help bring them closer to their own spiritual awakening. Not that any of this is wrong, but they can get so consumed with New Age terminology and techniques that they often miss the lessons they need to learn in order to strengthen their relationship with their soul self—God.

So what's the lesson? It is . . . *to be physical.* Yes, that means it's okay to have a healthy, vibrant sex life (I'm sure your other half is agreeing with me right now)! Furthermore, enjoy food and leisure activities in moderation, and find the balance between the serious-minded career person and the fun-loving, playful spirit. In order for you to fulfill your life path, you must maintain equality between your physical and spiritual needs, which will awaken you to the true purpose of your life and help you understand your relationship with your soul. As this happens, life works *for* you and no longer *against* you. Unfortunately, this doesn't mean that you won't hit a few bumps in the road, for that, too, is part of your growth process. Said in a more simplistic way:

*"Live from your heart, but allow your head to place
healthy boundaries."*
— The Guides

We can find examples of this throughout the world.
Take monks, for instance: On the surface, they may seem
to be denying their physical existence in order to concentrate strictly on their soul selves, but in actuality,
they're living life completely balanced. They take care of
their bodies instead of abusing them with inactivity and
the wrong types and quantities of food and drink—all the
while fine-tuning their soul selves on their chosen paths
to God.

Don't worry—you don't need to become a monk to
learn how to achieve this balance. The circumstances in
your life will let you know when you're out of sync. For
example, addictions and cravings are the results of an imbalance in you and your life, and they come in all colors and flavors. Some addictions are brighter and tastier
than others, but know that they're all caused by an imbalance. Does it surprise you that when you binge on
sugar, you then crave salt? Your body is telling you that
it needs to be balanced. But how? *Moderation!*

It's important to realize that when your physical
self takes over and says, "Ooh, I'm going to have some
of that chocolate cake," even though you know it will
cause an imbalance that could trigger a migraine
headache or send your blood sugar sky-high, it's hurting you *physically.* Again, the lesson is moderation—

that is, enjoying a slice without eating the whole darn cake. It's learning how to dabble in the physical pleasures without excess.

I have Crohn's disease, yet I crave all the foods that will trigger attacks. Does this stop me from eating the fried foods that south Louisiana is famous for, or eating the Cajun spices that come with most meals down here? I try, for a little while, but sometimes the cravings get the best of me. I'm human, and there's nothing like a good cup of gumbo followed by a dish of Louisiana bread pudding.

Unfortunately, we all have addictions that create imbalances in our lives. While we all have to *struggle with* something in our life, the key is to learn to *live with* it in our life.

● ● ●

I want you to think of an area of your life that's causing you distress. Do you overspend, overeat, overreact, or overwork? Make it a point to change this one area of concern for just one week, and notice the improvement that occurs. It's all about small successes and realizing that you have the ability to change how you treat yourself, both inside and out.

If you can do it for one week, you can do it for one month. If you can do it for one month, you can do it for one year. It will then become a positive pattern, leading to a permanent change in your life. Understand that the journey you follow, the skills you learn, and the confidence you gain along the way will all provide you with the wisdom and balance needed to embrace your spiritual self.

Finding balance in your life is a personal and individual journey, a process that requires that you constantly seek what works for you. You can start now by noticing the signs and/or symbols in your life, such as people you meet, music you hear, familiar objects that you use every day, and passages you read. This book, for instance, didn't appear in your hands accidentally. All the signs and symbols that come into your life can be used as messages from your spiritual self, your soul. By noticing them, by paying attention to the environment around you, and by embracing the seven insights in this book, you'll learn to recognize and understand the messages needed to find your balance. You'll start to hear your soul's voice and begin Cracking the Coconut Code.

Without a doubt, moving forward and transforming your life will come with struggles. But understand that your life is meant to be filled with love, joy, truth, and ultimately, peace. These seven insights will help you transform your life, much like they did for me, and hopefully lead to a deeper and more rewarding existence. In my search for their meanings, I found that the first symbol I was shown, the coconut, had a deeper significance than what I could have ever expected.

After interpreting and analyzing these insights, I re-named them so you could easily remember them. Thus, the first letter of each of the insights spells "C-O-C-O-N-U-T." So let's get started by learning the *7 Insights to Transform Your Life!*

● ● ●   ● ● ●

INSIGHT #1
Confront the Fear of Knowing Yourself

"When man no longer has to look into the face of another to see himself, it gives him a sense of peace, for he sees the face of who he truly is, not the face of who he feels he is. He then becomes more confident in embracing his feelings and instincts. It is then that he faces all aspects of who he is and no longer finds fear in the openness of that."

— The Guides

Mardi Gras is celebrated in various parts of the world just before Roman Catholics observe Lent, and it's known for a number of festive traditions including parties, balls, and parades. One thing that makes the celebration unique is that almost everyone wears a mask in the parades and at the gala events to disguise themselves so that they look entirely different from their everyday selves.

Of course Mardi Gras only lasts a few days, but when we continue trying to hide our identity from others and even ourselves, it's as if we never take the mask off. This prevents us from revealing our true self, and while that may be fun for Mardi Gras or Halloween, it's not practical for life.

The quote at the beginning of this chapter suggests that we shouldn't have to look to others to see who we are. Now one of the most difficult things for us to see is our true self or soul—we often spend so much time trying to hide our own shortcomings and imperfections that we fail to notice our true self. This creates an identity that builds up a thick barrier between our physical self and our spiritual self. The longer we wear that false identity or mask, the more it limits our ability to see our true self clearly.

Remember Jim Carrey's character in the movie *The Mask?* While the mask he wore initially offered him courage, it came with a great price. In the end, he realized that the identity the mask gave him was false, and he needed to focus on his true self. He came to understand that he had the courage within him all along—and once he acknowledged this, his life started to fall back into place.

When we become blinded by a false identity, we must begin to peel away the layers of the mask that once offered protection, for whatever reason, so that we can see who we are and what we've become. Only then can we truly display our true self and learn to trust who we are.

* * *

I encourage you to try the following exercise if you want to learn more about the type of disguise you wear when you encounter difficult situations. This exercise will provide some insight to help you begin to understand yourself better. Before beginning, I caution you not to overanalyze the question. This is an intuitive exercise, not an analytical one, so trust the *first* answer you receive.

Now, let's begin. If you can find a quiet space, great, if not, just try to focus on yourself for a moment. Silently repeat the question; then, once you receive the answer, open your eyes and read the interpretation for the color your soul has revealed.

EXERCISE

Imagine a rainbow. What is the prominent color that stands out? (red, orange, yellow, green, blue, or purple)? Note that each color has advantages and disadvantages.

INTERPRETATION

RED

Advantage: You appear positive and upbeat. You avoid painful confrontations.

Disadvantage: You fail to stand up for yourself or set your boundaries. You smile when you want to scream. All the while, the temperature is rising until you blow. When you do, you "see red." This usually creates guilt, which makes you feel selfish for defending yourself. It's a vicious cycle.

ORANGE

Advantage: You come across confident and sure of yourself and your opinions. You usually get the last word because people are intimidated by your passion.

Disadvantage: You overreact and can be a tornado, leaving behind a trail of disarray. Be careful not to let your strong opinions mask your insecurities.

YELLOW

Advantage: You're in control, thinking things through; you never overreact to a situation. Your strength is your ability to stand up to the test.

Disadvantage: You avoid your emotions. You never get out of your head because you overanalyze everything. You miss the best of life when you push away your sensitivity.

GREEN

Advantage: You work hard not to create conflict. As a result, you appear warm, friendly, and eager to please.

Disadvantage: You internalize your feelings. You can handle inner conflict, but you avoid external struggles at all costs. If pushed to the max, you charge like a bull.

BLUE

Advantage: You can see both sides of a situation. You defend your position methodically, making the point with facts, not feelings.

Disadvantage: You're afraid of letting go and expressing your true emotions. When pulled into your feelings, your sharp tongue can cut deep. This reaction is one you work hard not to expose too often, but when you do, you strike quick and clean.

PURPLE

Advantage: You withdraw so that you can compose yourself before doing or saying something you might regret.

Disadvantage: You talk yourself out of reacting by immediately "rising above it." The message you give yourself is, "I'm bigger than this—I won't let it get to me!"

● ● ●

Have you ever stopped long enough to look at a rainbow? Of course you have. I'm sure you've also noticed that it always has the same number of colors in the same order. While you've probably known the colors of a rainbow since first grade, it's actually a more complex composition of colors than you might think. In fact, this complexity ensures that no two people will see the same rainbow in the same manner.

This is no different from who you are; while everyone in your life has an opinion about you, the most important thing is the opinion you have about yourself. When you let other's opinions dictate to you who you are, you're creating more layers for your mask than you can possibly imagine.

You have to decide at this point whom you're going to live for—you, or someone else's opinion of you. If you can make the decision now to discover how you feel about yourself and how you want to see yourself, your journey will be more plentiful and your rewards more fulfilling. The people in your life will see the positive changes in you, and who knows? They may even be inspired to start removing their own masks.

So what color of the rainbow did you see? Did it hit home, and did it describe how you react to the world around you? Personally, I like this exercise and have used it in my lectures and classes many times. I've heard only a few participants say that it didn't ring true for them. But think back a few minutes to when you initially did the exercise. Did you pick the first color that popped into your head, or did you second-guess your choice and go for a more "logical" color? Remember, in order to begin the task of chiseling away at your mask, you must be truly honest with yourself and go with your first instinct.

When my husband, Jim, did the exercise, he immediately visualized green. After reading the interpretation, he had no problem relating to what it revealed. He was able to recall several incidents in his life when he became very "bullish" because he didn't confront an issue or situation when it occurred. Instead, he internalized his feelings, letting them fester within him.

When I did this exercise, on the other hand, I saw the color red. It certainly made sense to me because being confrontational is my worst nightmare. I always want peace; therefore, I'm very uncomfortable when I have to confront a person or situation and will avoid doing so at all costs. When I do face someone or something, my anger sometimes gets the better of me, and then I feel guilty about standing up for myself. Even though I'm now more comfortable with confrontation, it remains an issue for me. Nevertheless, I can now confront smaller issues so that I can confidently define my boundaries without feeling guilty. By doing so, I defuse their ability to become the larger explosions that I've always avoided.

This first insight, *Confront the Fear of Knowing Yourself,* has served me well so many times. Please know that you can repeat this exercise as often as you feel it's necessary. This first awareness of yourself is just the beginning. Think of it as a small fracture in your mask—now you must work to chisel away the rest of it.

As you practice living the seven insights in this book and progress toward Cracking the Coconut Code, you'll be able to see how removing just one layer of your mask will reveal different prominent colors in your rainbow, and you may see some of them if you do the exercise again in the future. As your awareness of yourself unfolds, you'll begin to see, and react to, life differently. You see, your goal with this exercise is to embrace the positive aspects of *all* the colors of the rainbow. As science tells us, when you see a rainbow, you're actually seeing sunlight (pure white light) that has been diffused by an outside element (raindrops, crystals, and the like). So, if you can embrace the positive aspects of each color in this exercise and blend them into your life, they'll surround you in pure white light.

As you know, life is an uphill climb, but with the right tools, the view along the way can be rewarding. It takes dedication, persistence, and hard work in order to begin Cracking the Coconut Code and enjoy the nourishment that you can receive from life. Since you picked up this book, you're most likely ready to begin making a lifestyle change that will ultimately help you hear your soul's voice. If you only address the superficial issues within yourself, you'll continue to add layers to your mask. In order to transform your life, you must remove the mask one layer at a time and learn to expose who you are behind it. Until you do so, you'll never fully be in touch with yourself.

This reminds me of something one of my clients shared with me. She'd been following The Guides' teachings for some time and was starting to become aware of her own inner voice. Over a period of two days, she incorrectly measured ingredients for meals that she was cooking. Since she'd become aware that all signs and symbols that occur in life can be interpreted as a message from her soul's voice, her inaccuracy with the ingredients sent up a red flag. She determined that she wasn't "measuring up" in some area of her life, but she simply couldn't identify where she was falling short.

One week later, it came to her: She realized that she wasn't giving her son the attention he needed; thus, she wasn't measuring up as his mother. For months, she'd been juggling several tasks and constantly felt pulled by her son. She spent her days trying to do what was so "important," while having to pacify her "needy" son in the process.

She came to the realization that this situation was identical to what her father had done to her when she was a child. He'd never fully stopped what he was doing to pay attention to her, and she'd resented it. Yet now, as an adult, she was repeating her father's actions by doing the same thing to her own child . . . and that certainly wasn't what she wanted for him.

I think that we all have patterns within us that mirror what our parents did to us—some are healthy and some aren't. (This "soul reflection" is something I'll discuss in the next insight.) At any rate, within a week of realizing this pattern, my client refocused her energy and rescheduled her days, reprioritizing and re-creating her life. Now she spends quality time with her son every day, and as a result, he's not so clingy and demanding. She was willing to face the hard truth, a process that started because she accurately assessed her life and accepted responsibility for her past. If she hadn't realized that the process of transforming her life began with her, starting from the inside out, she wouldn't have been perceptive enough to address the needs of others—her son, most of all.

If you're having trouble seeing your mask, look at the people in your life: the man sitting next to you on the bus, the child tugging at your hem, the woman sharing your cubicle, even the person sharing your bed. They represent a part of you—and while their opinions shouldn't influence who you are, their roles in your life should be seen as lessons to help uncover who you are.

I challenge you to remove your blinders and pay attention to life's messages. It's all about you: Everyone plays a part around you. Begin to confront who you are by first being honest with yourself and removing the mask you've grown so comfortable wearing.

Before we move on to the next insight, I want to share one more exercise, which will reveal what you're searching to find spiritually.

EXERCISE

Imagine that you're holding an old book in your hand. What color is the binding?

INTERPRETATION

Blue:	You want comfort.
Red:	You look for realness, aliveness, and passion.
Green:	You seek healing from yourself spiritually.

Yellow/ Gold:	You seek knowledge in understanding yourself.
White:	You seek oneness with God.
Purple:	You want to communicate.
Brown:	You want to find your purpose in life.
Black:	You crave silence and peace.

Daily Message

All experiences, interactions, and actions are lessons to help you discover who you really are. Give purpose to all that happens in your life. Identify the message.

Life Message

Life begins from within. Everything and everyone in your life brings you messages from your soul to encourage and help you learn about yourself. As you "confront the fear of knowing yourself," you accept responsibility for everything in your life—the good, the bad, and even the ugly. You must live each day knowing that your soul is directing your life and that all that takes place in it is a message from your soul. Every time you go over a hurdle or overcome a difficulty, you're removing layers that have kept you away from your true self. This is the true purpose of living a physical life. Once you become aware of this truth, it changes your entire life by bringing both meaning and purpose into it.

● ● ●　　● ● ●

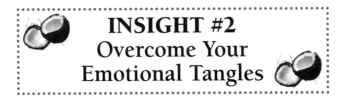

INSIGHT #2
Overcome Your
Emotional Tangles

"When man is emotionally tangled in life, a part of him is being suffocated that needs to be heard. The longer he avoids hearing the sounds of the tangle, the more difficult it is to clear. Eventually he is forced to confront the tangle by working through the emotional hardships that are created in everyday life. In removing each layer of emotional opposition, he exposes the true source of the tangle. By confronting these hidden emotions, he will begin to find balance with all."

— The Guides

Emotions aren't bad; in fact, they're necessary for healthy personal relationships. And when I speak of emotions in this book, I'm referring to the negative ones only. After all, who wants to overcome the good ones? Certainly not me. I encourage you to hang on to those positive feelings because they'll help you in this insight.

Emotional tangles are repeated patterns, the hurdles that keep you from living your life and moving forward. They're often manifested through past judgments, beliefs, prejudices, and "soul reflection." If not addressed, they'll continue to appear . . . and the longer you run from them, the more difficult they are to overcome. Recurring emotions will show themselves in different ways and will hinder your ability to create new, positive ones. The problem occurs when you have old feelings that continue to entangle you and prevent you from being able to interact with others in a peaceful manner.

Think back to the first insight and the story of my client and her son, whom she neglected because she'd fallen into the same pattern as her father. Her unresolved emotions caused her to unconsciously repeat a process that she hated. Once she owned her past, she was able to transform her negative childhood experience into a positive reflection. As a result, she reinforced her relationship with her son and can now look back at her own youth (with respect to this issue) with a sense of closure.

Judgments, beliefs, and prejudices are all formed from moments throughout our lives. Soul reflections, or behavior patterns, are what we receive from our parents, whether they manifest themselves in the ways we treat others, or in the ways we treat ourselves. These reflections reveal both healthy and unhealthy emotions—and, of course, the unhealthy ones are what we must overcome. If we hold on to the negativity surrounding them, rather than grasping their lessons, these emotions tend to recur. They'll eventually result in a tangle that we must unravel, which, unfortunately, can become so complex that it will continue to cause significant distress in our lives.

Think of an emotional tangle as an apple that's starting to rot: The decomposing part grows and starts to spread from the outside down to the core—if it isn't removed, it will spoil the entire apple. What may have started as a small area of discoloration becomes a large area of decay, making the apple inedible. Our recurring emotional tangles work in the same manner—what begins as a small area of interest eventually becomes a large area of concern. So if we ignore challenging feelings, they'll continue to grow and overtake our lives, resulting in a spoiled and decaying life.

Take criticism, for example, which is one of the most challenging issues for many of us. Some kinds are healthy, while other forms can be destructive and hurtful. Therefore, it's up to us to decide what we'll embrace and what we'll toss aside. We can't change what others might say—we can only change how we'll react to their words. In each instance, when we hear criticism, it's our choice to let our emotion create a tangle or a lesson. So, by conquering old feelings, we can remove another layer from our mask.

When I began doing my work, if someone told me that a reading wasn't accurate, I'd become devastated. It took me days, and sometimes as long as a week, to recover. I can remember cancelling appointments, swearing that I'd never do readings again. Even then, I knew what I was feeling would create a tangle that I'd eventually have to work at unraveling. After a few temper tantrums, I had to confront the truth: Why was I reacting so strongly to what others thought? Even though I wanted to wallow in my pity party as long as I could get away with it, deep down I knew that this was a reminder of what I'd endured as a child.

My family was bluntly honest, no matter what the situation or potential impact. Sometimes you just expect your family members to sugarcoat certain things; unfortunately, mine were, and still are, sugar free. This environment never allowed me to gain the confidence that I needed (or so I thought). My profession isn't a typical career, and my inability to separate myself from it made this criticism harder to swallow. I felt as though the judgment of my work was a judgment of *me*, but I now realize that this isn't true. I learned to understand that the criticism I endured growing up quite possibly "thickened my skin" to prepare me for what I'd encounter as an adult.

Coming to this realization took years, and during that time there was much disappointment thrown in my path. Even today, if someone criticizes my work or me, it hurts, but I don't hold on to the pain. I see it as an opportunity to learn another lesson rather than reacting negatively to an emotion that could become yet another layer on my mask.

So how do you overcome the rotten part of the apple? You address it by cutting out the decayed part, right? Well, you must do the same thing in your life: Overcome your emotional tangles directly by being completely honest with yourself about why you're reacting to a particular situation. Understand that feelings are natural, but how we react to them can have the greatest impact, both positively and negatively. Once you identify these emotional tangles, you need to get past them in order to be free to move forward. Unfortunately, doing so isn't easy—it takes courage, persistence, and a willingness to sacrifice your pride. So face it head-on and be willing to change and grow. In order to gain, you sometimes have to suffer loss . . . so let go of the rotten part of your apple.

In order for you to know how your spiritual self perceives the way in which you face your problems, try the following:

EXERCISE

Visualize a tree filled with apples. See yourself either hugging the trunk of the tree, sitting on one of the branches reaching for an apple, or sitting at the top of the tree enjoying the apple you've picked. Where do you see yourself in relation to the tree?

INTERPRETATION

— If you saw yourself **hugging the tree**, you tend to embrace problems head-on. You don't wait for things to get overwhelming or tangled; instead, you see it, embrace it, and fix it. Through your own readiness to take care of things, you may have little tolerance for how others handle their issues. "Get out of my way, let me do it! It's just quicker for me if I do it"—does this sound familiar?

— If you saw yourself **sitting on one of the branches reaching for an apple**, you acknowledge the problem, discomfort, or tangle, but so what? You'll get to it later. You don't want to face it yet . . . and this is what causes all emotional tangles to fester and grow. "I'll do it tomorrow" is your motto.

— If you saw yourself **on top of the tree**, you simply don't see that there's a problem: "Me? I don't have any tangles or problems. I'm fine." Unfortunately, with this attitude, the tree can rot out from underneath you before you know it, and then you'll fall on your butt. "I don't know what happened. I wasn't paying attention!" Can you relate to this?

● ● ●

A perfect example of unraveling emotional tangles occurred at one of my speaking engagements. There was a shy young woman seated in the last seat of the very back row. When it was finally her turn to ask a question, she said, "I'm so shy that it has hindered my life. I'm afraid to have friends, so I stay to myself. I'm so lonely and insecure. . . . I can't hold jobs even though I'm overqualified for most of them. There should be no reason why I can't do my job, but I get fired because my employers say I lack self-confidence. Why do I destroy everything good that comes to me?" she asked. "Why do I sabotage myself?"

Immediately, The Guides showed me the words *six years old.* I asked her what had happened when she was six to make her feel rejected. I got a typical "deer in the headlights" response: She just stared at me, unable to relate to anything I'd told her. This kind of reaction is very common in a group environment and certainly gives me no level of confirmation in what I'm seeing at the time, but being my determined self, I continued. I asked her again to think about what I was seeing. That's when she told me that she'd spent many years in therapy, yet she and her therapist had failed to uncover the event that could have caused her emotional trauma. I told her to think about it, because unraveling these emotional tangles is a process, much like Cracking the Coconut Code. It takes time.

Like so much of what goes on in my work, people don't always know what I'm talking about at the moment, but then in the middle of the night or a few weeks or months later, they suddenly remember something significant. In the case of the shy woman, it was at the end of the lecture—I didn't have to wait long for her memory to click in. As others were leaving, she waited to talk to me. She said that she'd been thinking about what I'd said during the rest of the workshop, and she finally remembered an incident that had happened to her at the age of six. (It always amazes me how the fragments of information The Guides give me often serve as stepping-stones for my clients to access their memories.)

I could tell that she was nervous and uncomfortable as she shared her recovered memory with me: When she turned six, her mother gave her a birthday party and invited her classmates and friends, but no one showed up. Even though this incident had devastated her, until The Guides got her attention, she'd been unable to remember it. This was such an awakening for her, and that's why I love what I do. In this case, as in so many others, it proves to me that my work makes a difference in someone's life.

That shy young woman had tucked the event and its emotions so far away that she'd truly forgotten what had happened to make her feel so inadequate and unacceptable. She couldn't realize, especially not at six years of age, how other people's opinions of her would make such a lasting impact on her life. Even though she'd only just remembered this painful event, it had been slowly eating away at her, from the outside down to her core, for many years.

This second insight, *Overcome Your Emotional Tangles,* is important in confronting your true self and getting to the milk in the coconut. While it may be easier to remain within the security of your routines and patterns, this can be destructive. Recurring feelings act like a disease: If untreated and allowed to fester over time, they'll consume you, leaving nothing healthy to share with others. So, start now by addressing the recurring feelings in your life. Know that you must unravel your emotional tangles if you want to begin Cracking the Coconut Code.

Thankfully, there are ways to overcome your emotional knots. You must acknowledge your feelings and study your reactions. Know what consumes you, and be more attentive about why you might react to a rather insignificant situation that may create judgmental and prejudiced behavior. This is part of understanding who you are, and this is when you'll see your life begin to change.

I encourage you to look around. Notice how you react to your family and friends at home and at work: Is there any consistency in your reactions? If so, this is a good place for you to confront and overcome your emotional tangles. Realize that you can't change the reason why you first experienced the emotion, but you can change the way in which you interact with the feeling *today*. Your feelings tell your story, for they're the tools that enlighten you about the secrets that live within. So breathe deeply, live your life, and embrace all that you are.

Daily Message

When difficulties arise, ask yourself these two questions: <u>*Why does it hurt? Why am I reacting?*</u> *By doing so, you can unravel emotional tangles and avoid creating new ones.*

Life Message

Always look at your emotions as a frontier to explore. Prejudices, judgments, beliefs, and soul reflections are emotional tangles that need to be unraveled. What shaped or caused these issues?

● ● ●　　● ● ●

INSIGHT #3
Claim Your Tools

*"In the world of man, all difficulties, hardships,
and lessons must be seen as useful tools that help
him chisel away the walls of separation he has created between himself and his higher guidance. By
identifying the purpose and learning of each, he will
see that the role they play in his life provides him
the necessary tool for his next lesson."*

— The Guides

The first two insights involved taking an inventory of your life by teaching you how to confront and overcome the issues that keep you from hearing your soul's voice. While they forced you to look at what was holding you back, the third insight prompts you to ac- knowledge the tools that life constantly provides you.

You see, every obstacle you encounter along your path is actually a unique device that's meant just for you. So when I say "claim your tools," I mean that you must decide how you'll face the hurdles in your life. By recognizing them as ways in which you can strengthen your resolve, you'll be able to face anything in life. And keep in mind that it's up to you to recognize the purpose of your tools—in other words, you must see each one as an opportunity for growth, no matter how difficult it may appear.

There are many obstacles in everyone's lives. By sharing examples of the heartache, the understanding, and the acceptance of several of my clients, I hope that you'll be able to see how roadblocks are actually useful for peeling away the layers of your masks. This is a difficult insight to embrace, but I never said that Cracking the Coconut Code would be easy!

So, roll up your sleeves and get comfortable—you're going to be here for a while. Realize that there *is* a light at the end of the tunnel, a silver lining to every dark cloud, and . . . sweet milk inside your coconut.

• • •

Unfortunately, one obstacle that many of us are aware of is abuse, and it's a very difficult one to comprehend. This story involves the molestation of two sisters by a family member. The abuse had gone on for several years before my client realized what was happening to her daughters. After she overheard one of their conversations, she confronted them. It was very surreal, and she couldn't believe what she was hearing. She and her husband then sat with their girls, cried, hugged, and tried to absorb the details.

I can't imagine how difficult this was for the entire family, yet they called and confronted the alleged abuser, an extended-family member. While he admitted to the molestation, he never apologized for his actions. Regardless of whether you view the tool as the abuser himself or as his actions, it matters not, for he did indeed serve as a sharp, pointed implement that cut through many layers of my client's mask.

I'm sure you're asking how the perpetrator could possibly serve as a tool for my client and her family. Well, since then, the two daughters have become parents themselves, and they're very protective of their own children, vowing to prevent similar actions from happening to them. The abuser served as a tool for them to be proactive for their children and prevent this pattern from continuing.

Likewise, the abuser served as a tool for my client, the girls' mother, to force her to learn how to forgive. On a soul level, this tragedy was necessary for her to develop a closer connection with God. Through her own faith, she accepted that God had a purpose for each experience in her life, even though the pain seemed unbearable at times. Had my client not realized this, she could have directed her anger toward the abuser, ultimately resulting in a destructive cycle of hate, and a loss of inner peace. Yet her faith empowered her to cut that rotten part of her apple out of her life. By forgiving the abuser of her little girls, she gained an appreciation for what God has to forgive every day. This took many years, but in the end it deepened her faith and allowed her to comfort and support others experiencing similar situations.

* * *

What I encourage you to understand is that while there are terrible things that happen in our lives, there are no victims. Everything that happens is a tool designed to get our attention and help us chisel away the layers of our masks between our God-selves and us.

I've had to learn to view my own obstacles as tools, but it hasn't been easy. I often find out about them through dreams, much like the one I'm about to share with you: I was standing in line waiting to be taken someplace special, but I didn't know why or with whom. Other people were around, but they were all ignoring me, except for two people who were definitely over-dressed for the occasion. They had flawless skin, crowns on their heads, and lips painted a passionate red. Unfortunately, I recognized these two people, and I wasn't happy to see them there because of the heartbreak they were causing my family during that time in our lives. Even in the dream, I could feel my heart hurting. They each pointed to the books that they were holding, which were marked *Special Lesson*. I knew then that they were *my* special lesson.

When I woke up, I realized that the heartbreak they were creating in my family's life actually represented tools to point out my own strengths and weaknesses. Very simply, the way in which they were dressed served as an important message for me: Their special attire, painted-red lips, and crowns on their heads highlighted the fact that I shouldn't overlook their purpose in my life.

Has it made it any easier for me to see these two as a tool I need in my life? Of course not! However, I now know that I have a lesson to learn, and in time, I'll be able to embrace the obstacle that they created for my family and me. Then, and only then, will I see this situation as an opportunity to learn a painful lesson.

If you can find the tools in the greatest of tragedies, then you'll be able to see them in the smallest of setbacks as well—and you'll be able to build on what comes next. This process takes time and practice, but you don't have to tackle all your obstacles at once, and you don't have to be perfect. This is a learning process, and even in your disappointments, there's something to be gained.

Remember, if you don't face your obstacles the first time, you'll continue to see them again and again. Claim your tools if you wish to get past them. This insight requires perseverance and commitment in order to get closer to Cracking the Coconut Code.

EXERCISE

Imagine a toolbox. In it are a hammer, a saw, a wrench, and a screwdriver—which one do you automatically reach for?

INTERPRETATION

— **Hammer:** This tool will help you stay focused on reaching your goal. This is also a "heads up" that your next lesson will be for you to finish what you start. You may have a tendency to get distracted or disillusioned too quickly. *Stay focused.*

— **Saw:** A saw is the perfect tool for your job—your soul's voice is telling you that you need to make a decision and let it go. You create problems for yourself because you're always questioning your decisions. Make your choice and move on.

— **Wrench:** To say that you can be a little too controlling for your own good is an understatement. You can expect your next lesson to be one that encourages you to let go of the reins and simply enjoy the ride. Remember, you don't want to drive—let someone else lead the way.

— **Screwdriver:** You can expect to be confronted soon with a situation that forces you to back off and slow down. This is so difficult for you because when you get your mind set on something, others need to get out of your way. You're like a dog chasing a bone—you simply don't give up. *Slow down.* Practice walking through something, and try not to run. This has always been a difficult tool for you to use.

Daily Message

Identify the tool(s) that are helping you remove the walls you've built between you and your soul. Find the "you" in your problems.

Life Message

Create what you need in order to be infused with life! Adopt the idea that God places all blessings and difficulties in your life to help you peel away the layers of the mask between you and your soul.

● ● ●   ● ● ●

INSIGHT #4
Offer Your Support

"It is not necessary for us to say that man's faith is his support. Man instinctively knows that God is the support of man. What is necessary, though, is that while here on Earth, man must know who and what supports and encourages him on his way back to his own Godliness. He must love himself enough to be truthful about what person, belief, or walk of life truly honors him, for it is impossible for man to grow when he does not know his support."

— The Guides

As you move through the insights of *Cracking the Coconut Code,* the fourth insight truly is a pivotal one, for it's the hinge that connects your spiritual and physical life. It's no coincidence that it's this middle insight that balances the demands of the spiritual and physical worlds. Up until now, you've been learning how to transform aspects of yourself that were internal, but this insight involves the external, or the balance between you and those around you.

Who you are and what you become depends on how you interact with others: how you allow them to affect your life, what you let them give you, and what you permit them to take from you. Life is all about give-and-take—so you must offer and accept support.

The old adage "No man is an island" is certainly true when transforming your life. You cannot live isolated from those around you because you'll never grow outside yourself, nor can you truly transform your life without the support and interactions of others. This fourth insight is asking you to depend on others to support you and to look outside yourself . . . and it's absolutely crucial.

• • •

We all have something to give that others need, and this is considered the purest form of charity. When we offer support to others—either those whom we love or complete strangers—we're giving away a part of ourselves, thereby removing yet another layer of our mask. Some will accept what we offer and some won't, but the only responsibility we have . . . is to offer what we have. It's in this offering that we grow. Likewise, when others extend to us what *they* have, it's our responsibility, not theirs, to know if we need it in our lives. If we do, then we must embrace and use it. If we don't, then we can either accept it to give to someone else, or simply discard it and move on.

I'll never forget an individual affectionately referred to as "Bubble-Gum Bill," an older man who passed out bubble gum to every fan at every game when my son played college baseball. Bubble-Gum Bill was one of the most recognized and appreciated fans at the game, and it was routine to seek him out and get a piece of gum. Even though the fans may not have chewed it, his offering was what made the two-cent piece of gum special. In fact, many of the adults would pass along their piece to children sitting nearby, and I promise you, these kids thought they'd hit the jackpot.

Thus, the value of the offer multiplied: One initial offer turned into a multitude of offers, and although it was just cheap gum, everyone was acknowledged and appreciated down the line. In other words, this man's gift offered the fans support, and in turn, their appreciation of him and his gift represented their support for him. He developed an identity that was appreciated and respected, and the fans had the pleasure of chewing gum during the games. (And that man sure loved being called Bubble-Gum Bill!)

• • •

When we have a common bond with someone, a support system is created between us. When that bond is no longer there, the relationship shifts or moves on. Many times this is exactly what happens when friendships change in some way, when jobs become boring, when we tire of our home or neighborhood, and when families grow apart. When there's no longer anything that connects us, the support system disintegrates. Fortunately, this doesn't have to happen—the bond can stay strong, but it takes a lot of hard work and effort.

It's important that you surround yourself with individuals who support your growth. Most important, know to whom you can go to in a time of crisis or need. Who is truly loyal to you? Who speaks the truth? Who will tell you what you need to know in the appropriate manner? Only then will you really know who *your* support system is.

It's also important that you be a source of support for others. If you're unclear about this, ask yourself the following questions: *Am I someone whom my friends can turn to? Am I a positive influence in the lives of others? Can others count on me in a time of crisis?* If not, make it a daily practice to give some part of yourself away to one in need. It can be in the form of a lent ear, a sincere compliment, or an encouraging word—but make sure that what you offer is genuine, and not a meaningless and selfish act.

In the beginning of my work, my support system was quite small, but very instrumental to my life path. As my work developed, so did my support. My readings provided help for others, but they also proved valuable for me. Even today, when I feel low, I ask for direction and a sign to confirm that I'm following the right path. It never fails: The next day my clients tell me how my work changed their lives or the life of someone they love. They tell me that they feel more alive in their hearts and that my work strengthens their own faith. This helps me to keep going, even when my path seems to be full of stones.

If you're unsure of the network you have in your life, try the following exercises, which will help you open your eyes to identify who your support system is and how they help you. (Write your answers on a separate piece of paper.)

EXERCISE #1

- *List ten people who are important in your life today.*

- *Next to each name, I want you to write <u>one,</u> and only one, word that describes each person. You'll need to listen to your intuition, your soul's voice, to receive your answers. For instance, what's the first word that pops into your head when you think of your best friend? If you got the word <u>funny,</u> then write it down beside the name.*

- *When you've finished the exercise, you'll be more clear on what each person offers you—good or bad. Be honest! This is the only way in which the exercise works.*

EXERCISE #2

- *Take the same list you made earlier, and next to each name draw a sun or a moon.*

- *For those who have a sun beside them, you still have light within you concerning them. You know that you want them in your life.*

- *For those with a moon beside them, you've put them to bed. They're no longer a part of your learning. It doesn't mean that they're no longer a part of your life; it just means that you've completed your learning with them.*

Now that you have a better picture of your support system, don't forget that the main person to whom you can offer support is *you*. Unfortunately, we often forget ourselves in this process. By embracing the first three insights of the Coconut Code, you're well on your way to supporting the person you know you can become. Get ready to soar!

• • •

Daily Message

Know your support. Know your truth. Live what you believe. Identify who or what encourages and strengthens you, and build on that every day. When all else fails, know who and what comforts you.

Life Message

You're a necessary part of God's plan. Regardless of what happens in life, never lose faith in yourself. Believe in you.

● ● ●　　● ● ●

INSIGHT #5
Nurture Your
Shortcomings

"It is truth: As man awakens to his spirituality, he awakens to himself. When he feels weakened by his shortcomings, he must learn to draw on his wisdom to accept what he is facing physically. Eventually he learns that by changing his feelings toward himself, he has more control over his shortcomings. That, my dear ones, is the defining step to become more spiritually evolved."

— The Guides

This powerful insight forces us to confront how we really feel about ourselves. Unfortunately, it can be unpleasant anytime we really engage in self-examination, which asks us to remove a layer of the mask. In the process, we may uncover many feelings about ourselves that have been tucked away, such as frustration, guilt, and low self-confidence, to name just a few. Such negative emotions are what I refer to as "shortcomings." If they're not identified and nurtured, then the external difficulties that plague us will continue in a repetitive pattern. Put another way, when we put too much of our effort into changing the external problem and not the internal one, conflicts and difficulties will keep appearing in our world.

When problems in our everyday life cause us stress or unhappiness, we reach out for help. This is when we start therapy, join a church, or find a support group. Fortunately, these routine challenges are excellent signs that there's a problem within us that needs to be addressed. This is also when we discover that we can *only* control what's within us; we have no control over what's happening outside us. In other words, only after we've recognized that the issues are within can we see how our external problems are actually shedding light on our shortcomings.

* * *

My workshops are often filled with a mix of people: There are men, women, mothers, daughters, fathers, sons, the single and the married; individuals of all professions; and there's a nice blend of those new to my work, as well as those more familiar with it. Even though the group is diverse, there's usually one thing that unites them: They all want to know the answer to a question or issue that's been troubling them. And if I can provide them with knowledge about themselves and their own journey, then the workshop is a success.

What's interesting, though, is that most of these concerns seem to be centered on struggles that the individuals are having in their everyday lives, issues that have caused enough difficulty that they wanted to come see someone like me. The question is usually something along the lines of, "I want to know how I can overcome the difficulty I'm having at work/with my relationship—will there ever be better times ahead for me?"

Unfortunately, these people often see things outside themselves as the problem, when in fact there may be an internal reason why they're in conflict. You see, we're all experts at finding our own faults. We may think that we're too fat, too brunette, too shy, too overbearing . . . the list goes on. If you picked "too brunette," then know that your shortcoming is actually that you're too self-critical. (I mean, do blondes *really* have more fun?) We begin to view these traits as weaknesses or limitations that hamper our ability to succeed in life. By doing so, we're allowing them to blind us to our abilities and our uniqueness. What we may see as a shortcoming can actually be an undeveloped strength. Remember, we're all perfect in God's eyes, and these perceived failings are nothing more than unique challenges to draw strength from and use for personal and spiritual growth.

Furthermore, seeing our deficiencies (which everyone has, including me!) as limitations keeps us alienated and isolated from our inner beauty. My *perceived* shortcomings have really helped me be who I am today. Recently, The Guides gave me a message in a class I was teaching on identifying and nurturing our weaknesses. Since I don't often get personal messages, I thought this was going to be fun.

The Guides said that I needed to overcome what was

robbing me of the life I needed to live. (Okay, this wasn't *that* much fun because it meant some self-reflection and work. Hey, I didn't pay to attend this workshop, so maybe I shouldn't be receiving a message. I wondered if I could give it back.) They said that I needed to learn how to love unconditionally. I didn't understand what this meant. How could I be a 57-year-old woman with a husband of 34 years and a 32-year-old son and not know how to love unconditionally?

At first I dismissed the message because I felt it was something that didn't apply to me—it must have been for the person in the front row. I'm the biggest skeptic in the room at any event, so I was happy to find a better home for this piece of advice. I thought that if it were really meant for me, something more clear would have come through. There, I passed that buck! Unfortunately, it didn't take long before that buck came right back to me. I received the same message in another class, but this time it had much more information. The Guides said, "This soul needs to learn how to love who *they are* unconditionally, and until this shortcoming is confronted, this soul will not be able to fulfill their soul purpose."

Hello! Now I knew that they were talking about me because this was dead-on accurate. My deficiency had nothing to do with how I love others; it had to do with how I view myself. The message went on to say that I'd learned to love my spiritual self, but I'd never learned to love my physical self. I knew that this didn't mean how I thought I looked in a red dress, but rather how I treated my body. The Guides were telling me that the time had come for me to practice what I preach. After all, in order for us to have complete balance and harmony within ourselves, we need to love ourselves completely. The physical body is a reflection of the soul—when it's not cared for in a healthy, loving way, it causes too much conflict in life.

Finally, I could relate to The Guides' message for me. I do very little for myself and have a hard time relaxing. My daughter-in-law finds it amusing that I'm the only one she knows who goes to a massage to get relaxed, only to leave more stressed than when I went in because I can't lie there for an hour. To make matters worse, I've been struggling with Crohn's disease for several years. It's the single greatest way to monitor my personal neglect—if I don't watch my diet and slow down, then it will slow *me* down in a very painful and uncomfortable manner.

Unfortunately, I needed this shortcoming (illnesses can indeed be viewed as such) to force me to take a look at, and take better care of, myself. Although my shortcomings may differ from yours, I'm sure that you can relate to The Guides' message as well. While we each try so hard to love others unconditionally, we often neglect ourselves. Maybe we should all make a bigger effort to stand at the front of the line instead of waiting for the leftovers.

● ● ●

I realize that it may be difficult for you to embrace your faults and accept that they've molded who you are. Even though you may want to ignore them, know that this isn't possible; you must *overcome* them. The best way to do so is to learn to nurture them, develop them, and view them as positive qualities placed in your life to strengthen you. If you can become more aware of your thoughts and emotions, particularly toward yourself, then your attitude toward life will be more optimistic.

Gradually distance yourself from those individuals who overwhelm you and prevent you from nurturing yourself. (You know the ones I'm talking about. These are the individuals in Exercise #1 of the previous insight who didn't make you smile when you thought about them.) Realize that if you constantly give to others and feel you get nothing in return, you'll grow angry and bitter. Work on saying no when you feel that something isn't in your best interests or when you don't want to do it. Selfish? You bet, and deservedly so. You've got to be selfish in order to protect yourself.

We all have shortcomings, but we must see the other side of them in order to appreciate their value in our lives. They can remove another layer of our mask—but in order for that to happen, we must work to embrace both the positive and the negative qualities of each one. For instance, my husband has difficulty finishing what he starts. He gets halfway through something and decides that it no longer intrigues him, so he becomes bored. Then, off he goes to create a new project. Unfortunately, this leaves a trail of unfinished projects, like bread crumbs, behind him. There's the weakness. On the positive side is a man who has great ideas and is quick to solve most problems . . . as long as he has someone behind him to clean up and finish what he starts. There's the strength. This shortcoming of his makes me crazy, but I do value his creative abilities as well.

Jim also refuses to allow someone else's opinion of him to influence the one he has of himself. I admire this trait—and should probably take notes—but to me, this is one of his shortcomings. While this positive side of him is one that I truly admire, the negative side is his inability to accept *my* constructive criticism. He thinks he's fine the way he is—period. So, my advice to him is to find a balance, especially when it concerns opinions that I need him to hear. Notice that I've shared Jim's faults with you and have respectfully declined to reveal all of mine, but I challenge you to identify and nurture your own.

You must know that life is more than what you see around you. Even though you see the stars at night or hear the wind that blows or feel the sunshine on your face, you may not understand the mystery and wonder of it. But you must trust that it's as important as the air you breathe, for everything in your world has a purpose—even your shortcomings. When you embrace that truth, you begin to value the treasures within you.

If you feel that you need help identifying a few of your weaknesses, try the exercise on the next page.

EXERCISE

Choose a quiet place (such as a peaceful room, a bathtub, or a corner of your garden) and grab a pencil. Read through the entire exercise first, then take a few deep breaths to center yourself and connect to your soul's voice. Now do the following on a separate piece of paper:

- *What parts of you would you like to give away? List them.*

- *Now, what parts of you would you choose to keep? List them next to those that you'd be willing to give away.*

INTERPRETATION

The purpose of this exercise is to identify those aspects of yourself that you see as strengths and those you see as weaknesses. The parts of you that you want to keep, naturally, you perceive as your strengths. The parts that you were willing to give away are what you see as your weaknesses. Remember, shortcomings are necessary for growth, but they don't need to hamper your progress.

Use this exercise as an opportunity to highlight areas that need nurturing. It's easy to remain so focused on your perceived faults that you never move forward; instead, you keep mulling over them but fail to realize why they're actually in your life. So, name those aspects of yourself that you see as weaknesses. Learn to nurture them and bring them to life. Give them an identity. Make them work for, not against, you. Use them to become stronger, more resourceful, and more successful. The lessons you learn in the process of facing your perceived deficiencies help define who you are and what you can become.

Now that you've identified these areas, use the following tips to understand why they're in your life. Find yourself in your shortcomings, and develop them into something that will further your growth and enrich your life.

- Become aware of who and what you criticize, including yourself.

- Work to find something positive in your weaknesses—that is, what can they do to inspire, motivate, or create new opportunities for you?

- Give your shortcomings life by giving them a name. See them not as something to hide, but as something to uncover.

Daily Message

When you ask, "Why God, why?" understand that these problems, limitations, or shortcomings are keeping you from truly tuning in to the real you, the true voice of your soul. Do your homework—what are you avoiding seeing in yourself?

Life Message

Your shortcomings are your perceived deficiencies and weaknesses. Work to change your perception of them from a negative to a positive reality. Don't run from your shortcomings; turn and face them. By avoiding who you are, you're dismissing the unique aspects of yourself.

• • •   • • •

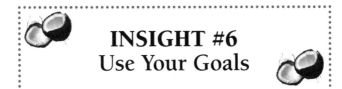

INSIGHT #6
Use Your Goals

"When you lose focus in your life, you walk through life with blinders, for you lessen the power of your truth. You stagger upon Earth. Your direction becomes cluttered. You are unable to feel the power of your own Godliness. Focusing on the outcome, in both the physical and the spiritual, will lead you back in to your truth."

— The Guides

In everything you do, there's a beginning and an end, or a desire and a goal. Most failures are the result of a lack of focus. Think of it as the headlights on a car as you drive through a rainstorm—the beams from the headlights are all you can see. Yet in order to drive through the storm safely, you must look straight ahead and follow the lights without allowing anything to distract you from reaching your destination. If you lost your lights, you'd lose sight of the outcome (the goal), increasing the chance that you'd get in an accident. It's the same thing in your life: If you fail to see the end result, you increase the likelihood that you'll fall short and miss your desired aim.

As you can imagine, there have been many times during my years of learning that I could have lost sight of my goal, which was to sharpen and strengthen my intuitive abilities. If I'd lost my focus, I never would have been able to reach the goal I'd set for myself. There have been times that I've temporarily lost my focus, but each time, I encountered difficulties that quickly got me back on track.

Keep in mind that we all have rainstorms that we must get through in order to reach our goals. They give us strength and test our resolve, and in order to overcome them, we must maintain our focus. Whether the goals are daily or lifelong, focusing on the outcome will keep us steady and help us weather the storm.

One of my storms occurred a few years ago—although it felt more like a destructive tornado at the time. A professor at a local university asked me to speak in front of one of his classes that had been studying the area of metaphysics. Before speaking, he asked if I'd go into an altered state to give personal messages to the class. What he failed to tell me was that he'd also invited his religious-studies students. When I walked into the room, people were lined up, wall-to-wall. I was excited to see such a profound interest in my work . . . in fact, I wondered if I was actually in the southern Bible Belt. Unfortunately, it didn't take long for me to find out what was really going on.

I spoke for a few minutes about who I was, what I was about, and what I was going to do. To say that I was a little naïve back then is a huge understatement. But looking back, I realize that this experience turned out to be one of my "tools"—a hurdle that I needed to learn from, and I did just that in a big way. After all, these tools aren't always easy to use. . . .

Anyway, when I finished delivering The Guides' messages, I opened my eyes to a room full of skeptics. The professor found a seat on the floor behind me, and that should have been my first clue that the guns were going to start firing. In an abrasive manner, one of the students who received a personal message confronted me. He bluntly said, "Lady, I don't know what you're missing in your life, but it's obvious to everyone in this room that you're a con artist."

Of course, my reply was, "I'm sorry you feel that way. I know my work is valuable to many."

"That is exactly what a con artist would say," he retorted.

I was devastated, to say the least. I'd gone there with high hopes that the students really wanted to learn about my work, and I was excited to share my gift with them. Unfortunately, that student's comments issued an invitation for the rest of the nonbelievers in the class to share their opinions on my work—and their feelings about me. I didn't really want to know what they thought of me, and I desperately wanted this experience, which turned into 45 minutes of pure hell, to end.

Why do our lessons have to be so hard? It wasn't fair, because had I known the format, I wouldn't have put myself in that situation. And a friend who accompanied me that day later told me that if she'd had my gift, she would have hidden it under a bush a long time ago. Had it not been for my husband and son, I would have thrown in the towel and allowed what happened to push me out of my line of work.

Fortunately, I've persevered over the years. If that kind of thing were to happen to me today, I'd exit the room with my head held high, knowing that my work brings much peace, comfort, and direction to many. It would still hurt, but not to that degree. In fact, there's another professor at that same university who still invites me to speak to his classes. (Of course, the first time I went back, my son insisted on going with me to protect me just in case there was another feeding frenzy. Thankfully, all went well.)

• • •

Bhrett, my son, also had to learn how to use his goals to keep him focused in life. He started college with open ambitions, but wasn't exactly sure what he wanted to do, which is a common dilemma. So near the end of his undergraduate work, he decided to pursue a degree in psychology. However, he realized that this would require a doctorate because a bachelor's degree in that particular major doesn't guarantee a great job.

Once he entered graduate school (not a small feat, but it really seemed to click for him), the process took a great deal of time. After five years, he left for his internship but still hadn't completed his dissertation. To make matters worse, he was moving to a different state without any plan to complete this final stage.

As the year passed, Bhrett realized that he needed to refocus on the outcome or he was going to lose all that he'd worked for up until that time. Perhaps the thought of moving made him realize that he needed to finish his project or he could easily lose sight of his goal. Finally, he completed his dissertation, but not without having to refocus on his project. He wasn't willing to lose all that he and his family had invested and accept that he'd fallen short of his goal. It wasn't without difficulty, but he believed in this process and in his resolve, and he kept his focus on the outcome, the ultimate goal.

Just like my son, you must keep your focus on the light at the end of the tunnel. The following will help you remove a layer of your mask by revealing what keeps you from reaching your goals:

EXERCISE

On your mental screen, visualize a backyard with a sand-box, a bicycle, and a swing set. Do you want to play in the sandbox, swing on the swing set, or ride the bicycle around the block?

INTERPRETATION

— **Sandbox:** Since you constantly change your goals, soon forgetting the ones you made yesterday, it's extremely hard for you to reach them. Begin setting daily objectives for yourself. This will not only help you stay focused, but it will give you an added bonus: You'll begin to see the miracles of success!

— **Bicycle:** You reached the aims you set for yourself long ago, but you've never noticed your success. You stay so busy that you keep working on the same issues—it's time to notice your accomplishments. You set the goals, you just forget to notice when you've met them. Wake up and smell the success!

— **Swing Set:** Goals—what are they? You don't want to be bothered with the details. You learned early on that the best way to deal with life was not to set yourself up for disappointment. Your attitude is simply to take whatever comes. Begin to change this approach by setting one reachable goal a week. This will change your life!

My copy editor chose the swing set in this exercise, and the message it held for her really hit home. She said, "I have no problem helping others reach their goals—I just don't want to set myself up for failure. So if I don't have any personal goals, I won't have any personal failures." While she feels that she's protecting herself from failure, in reality she's failing herself by not setting any personal goals.

So, how did you do? Do you agree with the exercise's interpretation? If not, spend time thinking about your life to see if you have dreams that haven't been accomplished. This is a great exercise to do when you feel that your life has no focus, or when you're having difficulty understanding what you want in life.

Focus on everything you want to accomplish daily, weekly, monthly, and yearly. Then, use your abilities to meet the goals that are important to you. When you feel that you're in control of your life, your future is solid. *Use Your Goals* is the insight that will help you create the future you need in order to be successful in hearing the voice of your soul. Soon you'll be able to taste the milk in the coconut!

Daily Message

Set daily, reachable goals—and be persistent. Live your life as though you're one step closer to the big prize.

Life Message

Keep your eye on the light at the end of the tunnel. After all, there's a goal to reach! Don't let anyone or anything keep you from following the path of hearing your soul's voice, which is the voice of God.

● ● ●   ● ● ●

INSIGHT #7
Trust the Process

*"Looking into your past to see how much you have
accomplished in this life will give you the confidence
to continue forward in your growth. But not until
you see yourself as being strong will you be able to
accomplish your soul's goals and live wholly in your
life. Our purpose as teachers is to help awaken you
to your truth, to teach you how to become aware of
what is important to you and what your values are.
These are important lessons for you to learn."*

— The Guides

You need to trust yourself in order to live the life that
your soul desires. Until you do, you'll never fully
reach your potential, and you'll always doubt whether
you deserve what comes your way. So, live what you
want to become. You came into this life with a spiritual
path to follow in order to accomplish your soul's goals.
It's important for you to reach those goals, but it's more
important that you recognize that the journey you've
taken to attain them is the learning, not the outcome.
Let go and live through them. Let life happen.

The final insight of *Cracking the Coconut Code* could

not be any truer for my life—after all, I started on this path without much understanding of where I was going. If I'd chosen to be a pharmacist as a child and gone to pharmacy school, it would have been easier to think of a career path and lifestyle to follow. It may not have come true, but at least I would have had a road map to follow. Instead, the journey I've taken has been one through uncharted territory. I've had to learn to trust my skills, my faith, and ultimately, my life path. I admit that I had to do this kicking and screaming, crying and cursing, and laughing and shaking. But with all the trials and tribulations, I'm thankful that I trusted my path because of the lessons I learned along the way.

I have faith in what God has led me to do: I trust the information I receive, trust that it pertains to my client, and trust that it's meant to heal and not hurt. Since this process started, I've made many changes, but I believed that the purpose was to grow personally and spiritually. I believed it so much that I've opened myself to skepticism and criticism every day of my life.

I opened an office in a town ruled by strong, organized religious faiths—a town that was once home to some well-known evangelists. Yet I knew that doing so would provide me with a venue to teach, and that it would be a place for my own personal growth. I trusted it so much that I opened this office and didn't advertise, didn't have a standing appointment list, and didn't have a financial backer. I believed that if I were sincere in my efforts, it would all work out. I trusted that I would have the means to keep my office open and continue to expand my institute. As I said before, it hasn't been easy, but it's been educational.

Finally, I believed in myself enough to write this book and share information with those who may be interested. I once again opened myself up for criticism and ridicule because I felt that I had something to say. I trust that my story will be helpful in applying the seven insights to transform your life. Sure, I could have stayed in my comfortable world with my safe clientele and friends and kept doing what I was doing—but I had faith that my journey has brought me to the point in my life path where I'm ready to share the secrets of *Cracking the Coconut Code*.

So, trust yourself. Believe that you're ready to begin cracking the code, ready to reach for the treasure inside that tough husk, and ready to sample its sweetness. Have confidence that you have the insights to work through the difficulties and overcome the barriers as you continue to grow physically and spiritually.

Of course you can expect to go through periods in your life that will test your trust. Sometimes when life doesn't turn out the way you want, you may be quick to say that you must have done something wrong. In actuality, you probably did most things *right*. Now if you're old enough to read this book, you're old enough to know that life isn't always fair. During such times, you may find yourself wanting to escape the rat race and move to a cabin on top of some mountain someplace far away. I know that I do.

Well, life isn't always fair, but it *is* balanced. What we put out comes back to us—we can throw as many screaming fits as we want, but it won't change that truth. Unfortunately, we don't always know what our soul has planned for us to work through or overcome, and we don't always know what the lessons are, but we must trust that there will come a time when all debts are paid.

● ● ●

Recently, one of my clients made me laugh when she said that her life was running so smoothly that she was afraid to know what her soul had planned for her next that would mess it all up. She said, "Don't tell me anything—I don't want to know. Just let me enjoy how good this space feels a little longer." I seriously doubt that I could have told her anything that would have taken away her peace. Life *does* give us a breather every once in a while. . . .

Regardless of the treasures you have in life or the burdens you carry, it's your responsibility to make the best of the situation. So be true to yourself and believe that it will all make sense someday. As I've said many times, "God gives us the strength and courage to face whatever obstacles are in our paths. All we need to do is push up our sleeves and get to work." To trust *that* truth every day isn't always easy, but I know you have the courage, strength, and wisdom to do it! What are you waiting for?

Daily Message

Own your life every day, and live it! Don't <u>make</u> it work— <u>let</u> it work!

Life Message

Live what you believe, and trust yourself. If you concentrate on doing that, life works for, not against, you.

● ● ●   ● ● ●

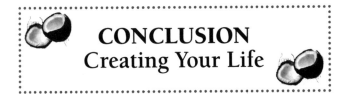

CONCLUSION
Creating Your Life

*"As life leads you into yourself, you become
aware that you cannot control any part of your
life outwardly, only inwardly. As you awaken,
you gradually accept the power from within.
You no longer search for the face of God
in another, but in the face of you."*
— The Guides

The most important piece of advice I can give you is to have faith that God is always with you, bringing you the lessons you asked to learn so very long ago. And when you begin to integrate the seven insights in this book into your daily life, you'll find that they're all connected, offering you help during all the many times you wondered "why."

However, you need to keep in mind that this is a *life* practice—in other words, you won't wake up one morning and have all the answers. Instead, what will happen is that you'll begin to see where you once stood and how far you've come. You'll recognize the transformation. When you practice these seven insights, you'll create a life that's produced, directed, and performed by your soul. You'll no longer be able to say, "I don't understand." Rather, you'll be able to get your own messages and use the people in your life to help you hear your soul's voice—and you'll be the one controlling the volume. The patterns in your life will begin to change, and you'll begin to heal . . . as I have.

•   •   •

A few years ago, I asked to understand why I always feel guilty for things that happen in my life. For example, I always feel regret for creating conflict whenever I stand up for myself. Even if I'm right, I feel wrong. I blame myself for everything.

A dream I had around this time really shocked me; it certainly ripped off a layer of my mask and exposed a situation from long ago. In the dream, I was four years old, playing with my cousins at my grandparents' house after a typical Sunday family meal. As always, the kids escaped from the eyes of the adults by slipping off upstairs to play, and on this particular day, we were all eating red apples. Our parents repeatedly told us not to throw the peels on the floor because someone would slip and fall. In the dream, I saw my grandmother walk into the room, slip on an apple peel, and break her hip.

The adults all ran upstairs to help her while they waited for the ambulance to arrive. And to say that they were upset was an understatement. Immediately, they started interrogating us kids, because one of us needed to be punished. In my dream, it felt as if I were back in my four-year-old body, experiencing all the same feelings I had that day. Everything seemed real: I could hear and feel what was happening, word for word, moment by moment; I could see the adults' frantic faces in detail as they kept asking whose apple peel had caused the accident; and I could feel how scared I was. But more important, I silently wondered if the apple peel was mine. In the dream, I felt that it was my fault that my grandmother had broken her hip.

I woke up in a cold sweat. Suddenly, it was so clear to me—my prayers had been answered. I now knew why I always blamed myself for everything. This dream replayed an actual memory that I'd tucked away as a child, and it was the key to why I always feel guilty. I remembered being afraid to speak up and say that I didn't know if it was my apple peel, so I privately took the blame. To make matters worse, my grandmother's health began to decline after that incident, and she died shortly thereafter.

I realized that I'd carried around this heavy load my entire life. It was then, at four years old, that I'd begun to shield myself from my true emotions, protecting my physical and spiritual self. In essence, I was starting to build the layers of a mask that I'd wear for many, many years. Yet as I practiced the seven insights contained within this book, I learned to slowly remove the layers of my mask to reveal these emotions and transform my life. It was necessary for me to deal with this experience before I could understand my issues with guilt and, ultimately, could move on with my life.

Remember, I was the one who asked to be shown why I'd always been plagued with guilt. I asked, and I received. So when *you* ask, be ready to get the answer. You hold the keys to your past, to your present, and to your future. When you allow these seven insights into your everyday life, you also bring your spiritual life into your physical life. (And, on a spiritual level, you've known these insights from day one.)

I want you to try the following exercise to see how what you've done here is working in your life. For 21 days, I want you to ask for guidance on whatever you need in your life—clarity, patience, humility, money, relationships, and so on. Then, at the end of each day, I want you to journal what went on around you: Who influenced you? What did they have to say? How did you react? What did you gain from the encounter? All you have to do is ask, but you must be prepared to receive. Your soul has a voice . . . so listen. It's always been there, and it always will be.

But, first things first: Do you think you know the code to cracking the coconut? If not, keep reading.

Confront
Overcome
Claim
Offer
Nurture
Use
Trust

In order to get to the top, you have to start at the bottom. Now you've broken the code!

Trust the Process to find your milk.
Use Your Goals to stay focused.
Nurture Your Shortcomings to empower yourself.
Offer Your Support to encourage yourself.
Claim Your Tools to remove the layers.
Overcome Your Emotional Tangles to satisfy your thirst.
Confront the Fear of Knowing Yourself by going within.

Please understand that while you read this book, you had to grasp the insights in the order that they were presented to me. It was only after working to understand them that I realized that once you learn them and are ready to begin transforming your life, you must then apply them by starting at the bottom and working your way up.

For example, I want you to think back to the story of my client and her son from the first insight. By paying attention to the signs and symbols in her life, this woman was able to recognize her message. She was able to *trust the process*. She then had to focus in order to understand what the message meant—she had to *use her goal* of finding her answer to keep her focused. Once she realized that her message was that she wasn't measuring up as a mother, she had to *nurture this shortcoming* to fix this issue in her life. Instead of criticizing herself, she chose a more active role and offered herself support to tackle the situation. By *offering support* to herself, she was ultimately able to offer the same to her son.

By embracing these insights, she was then able to *claim this event as a tool* in her life and grow from it with an awareness that would help her *overcome her emotional tangle*. By accepting this lesson, she could see that this pattern had started long ago with her father. Being able to understand this and change the pattern in her son's life gave her the strength and acceptance to let go of something that had occurred when she was a child. By correcting this pattern in her life and in her son's future, she was equipped to correct this in her past. Once she healed this part of her, she could *confront herself* and be proud of what she saw.

• • •

You must see the bigger reason for everything that happens in your life, but don't go overboard. Even though there's a private message in everything that happens to you each day, just live your life and don't make it hard. Take what you learn from interacting with others, and apply it to find your way. When you can do this, you'll have come full circle. You'll begin to live within your own counsel, and you'll know that when you look outside yourself, you're just seeing another view of you. You can no longer blame others for your life.

This book is a circle of life's journey . . . your journey. Adopt these insights as a way of life, and you'll hear your soul's voice, God's voice.

• • •   • • •

AFTERWORD

First, and foremost, you must understand that this is a reference book. It's meant to be a learning manual for you to use daily, in order for you to know the real you. If you're facing a situation that you're unsure of, ask for guidance, and then open the book to a random page. If the book opens to Insight #5— Nurture Your Shortcomings, then realize that you may need to find your shortcoming in the situation and work to resolve it.

Keep this book on your nightstand, in your car, on your desk, or even in your bathroom. Use it as a mouthpiece for your soul. It works!

• • •   • • •

ACKNOWLEDGMENTS

I want to thank Michelle Blazier and Flory Reynolds for their editorial support throughout the writing of this book. Both of them have been valuable resources to share ideas with. I still wonder how they managed to catch my words as they flew from my mouth. They somehow got most of them and found a way to organize them in some order.

Michelle, I couldn't have done it without you. Thank you for the extra work and time you put in away from your son and husband to see this project come to completion. Flory, thank you for being the teacher you are—you truly are my guardian angel. Because of the two of you, this book progressed from an idea to what it has become.

I also want to acknowledge Misty Martin, my office manager, for her willingness to schedule time in my day to devote to writing this book. It's not easy to keep me to a schedule, but without her perseverance, I never would have met the deadlines on this book. Misty, thank you for being the best assistant anyone could ever hope for and a special friend who goes the extra mile.

In addition, I'd like to thank Andreé Boyd, a friend for many years, who worked with me on earlier books and who helped me formulate what we've summarized here. To Hank Mendheim, thank you for taking the time to read the manuscript. I treasure your friendship.

John Edward, I thank you for believing in my work and giving me this opportunity to share it with a much larger audience. I'm grateful for your support and truly feel blessed to know you. Thank you!

I want to acknowledge my mother; my twin sister, Jean; and my sisters Joy and Ann. I love all of you. Bhrett, how could I ever thank you for choosing to be my son this time around? Without you, I never would have met The Guides. You've always been my biggest supporter and fan, even when it would have been easier for you to walk away from my work. What a trip this has been for you! I appreciate all your effort and work in helping me say exactly what needed to be said on these pages. Your connection with The Guides goes without saying. And Missy, thank you for loving him as much as you do and giving me two beautiful grandchildren. You are a godsend.

Last, thank you, Jim, for walking this journey with me. You've always been there without question. You're my blessing in every way.

● ● ●   ● ● ●

ABOUT
THE AUTHOR

Mary Jo McCabe is a respected and sought-after intuitive interpreter who receives symbols and messages from an individual's inner voice. She's developed a unique ability to communicate with individual souls, both living and deceased. Mary Jo offers personal insight, self-direction, and purpose through her communication with a group of spiritual teachers who refer to themselves as "The Guides."

Mary Jo focuses her work on helping individuals expand their awareness to understand, create, and evolve during their journey of life. She feels that her spiritual gift can provide the tools, techniques, and enough personalized information to ultimately teach her clients how to get in touch with their soul's voice. This will enable them to begin to find their own answers and enrich their lives. She feels that her work helps her clients understand themselves, their families, and their purpose in this life. As she says, "I help people open their eyes to what's right in front of them."

Mary Jo's intuitive translations and interpretations in the focused area of soul readings transcend to those souls who have passed on to the Other Side. Through this, she's able to connect clients not only to the spiritual readings of their life path, but also to messages and connections with those no longer on the physical journey. This often offers healing and allows loved ones to reconnect and to better understand death and loss.

Since 1987, Mary Jo has conducted thousands of individual soul readings through her work as the chairperson and leading founder of The McCabe Institute. Individuals from all walks of life seek to utilize Mary Jo's gift as an interpreter for their soul and their guides, as well as to access her intuitive abilities to gain greater insight into their lives. She has authored *Learn to See: An Approach to Your Inner Voice through Symbols, Come This Way: A Better Life Awaits,* and *It All Begins Here: Interpreting Your Dreams.* She's also created Symbol Cards as a tool to help her clients sharpen their own intuition and begin to hear their own soul's voice. (Also, psychic medium John Edward recommends Mary Jo McCabe as an intuitive in his book *One Last Time.*)

Mary Jo's home is in Baton Rouge, Louisiana, where she lives with her husband, Jim. Their only child, Bhrett, is married to Melissa, and they have two wonderful children, Logan and Caroline.

If you wish to contact Mary Jo, please call her office: (225) 926-3355; or visit **www.maryjomccabe.com.**

• • •   • • •

NOTES

NOTES

NOTES

NOTES

NOTES

NOTES

We hope you enjoyed this Princess Books publication.
If you would like more information about Princess
Books, you may contact the company through their
distributor, Hay House, Inc.:

Hay House, Inc.
P.O. Box 5100
Carlsbad, CA 92018-5100

(760) 431-7695 or **(800) 654-5126**
(760) 431-6948 (fax) or **(800) 650-5115 (fax)**
www.hayhouse.com

• • •   • • •

Distributed in Australia by: Hay House Australia Pty. Ltd., •
18/36 Ralph St. • Alexandria NSW 2015 • *Phone:* 612-9669-
4299 • *Fax:* 612-9669-4144 • *E-mail:* info@hayhouse.com.au

Distributed in the United Kingdom by: Hay House UK, Ltd.
• Unit 62, Canalot Studios • 222 Kensal Rd., London W10
5BN • *Phone:* 44-20-8962-1230 • *Fax:* 44-20-8962-1239 •
www.hayhouse.co.uk

Distributed in the Republic of South Africa by: Hay House
SA (Pty), Ltd., P.O. Box 990, Witkoppen 2068 • *Phone/Fax:*
2711-7012233 • orders@psdprom.co.za

Distributed in Canada by: Raincoast • 9050 Shaughnessy
St., Vancouver, B.C. V6P 6E5 • *Phone:* (604) 323-7100 •
Fax: (604) 323-2600